The ONE YEAR® MINI
FOR
Moms

The ONE YEAR® MINI

FOR
Moms

Tyndale House Publishers, Inc.
Carol Stream, Illinois

Visit Tyndale's exciting Web site at www.tyndale.com

TYNDALE is a registered trademark of Tyndale House Publishers, Inc.

Tyndale's quill logo is a trademark of Tyndale House Publishers, Inc.

One Year is a registered trademark of Tyndale House Publishers, Inc.

The One Year Mini for Moms

Designed by Beth Sparkman

Edited by Karin Stock Buursma

ISBN-10: 1-4143-0884-1
ISBN-13: 978-1-4143-0884-5

Printed in China

12 11 10 09 08 07 06
7   6   5   4   3   2   1

❀ ❀ ❀

TO MY BROTHER AND SISTER-IN-LAW,
DAVE AND ALICE BANKS:
Thanks for letting me stay in your Florida condominium
while I worked on portions of this book. Palm trees . . .
Intracoastal Waterway . . . eighty-degree weather . . . It was
a wonderful week! Your hospitality and generosity warmed
my heart.

TO MY EDITOR, KARIN BUURSMA:
When Tyndale House asked me to write these devotionals,
I immediately requested that you be my editor. Working
with you for the second time, I appreciated the same
qualities I had observed in you earlier. You are gracious,
straightforward, encouraging, and insightful—all at the
same time.

ELLEN BANKS ELWELL

God's Truth Works in Our Hearts

GOD'S PROMISE

Therefore, we never stop thanking God that when you received his message from us, you didn't think of our words as mere human ideas. You accepted what we said as the very word of God—which, of course, it is. And this word continues to work in you who believe. *1 Thessalonians 2:13*

❀ Whenever I enjoy a cup of cinnamon-plum tea, I steep a tea bag in piping hot water for several minutes. During that time, the flavors inside the tea bag saturate my mug or teacup. God's Word is like that. When we allow his Word to permeate our hearts—or the hearts of our children—he infuses us with his love, peace, wisdom, and power.

PRAYER

Father, thank you that when the truth of your Word permeates our hearts, it continues to do its good work. Amen.

Direction for My Confusion

GOD'S WISDOM

Trust in the LORD with all your heart; do not depend on your own understanding. Seek his will in all you do, and he will show you which path to take. *Proverbs 3:5-6*

Who are those who fear the LORD? He will show them the path they should choose. *Psalm 25:12*

Your word is a lamp to guide my feet and a light for my path. *Psalm 119:105*

❈ The places we seek direction for *our* lives influence where our children will seek direction for *their* lives. God's Word assures us that the best way to find direction is through *trusting* the Lord, *depending* on his understanding, and *seeking* his will in all that we do. All three of these things focus on him!

PRAYER

Father, I want to trust you and ask you for help—before I do anything else. Thank you for being eager to give me direction. Amen.

Keep the Big Picture in Mind

GOD'S CHALLENGE

Whatever you do or say, do it as a representative of the Lord Jesus. . . . Work willingly at whatever you do, as though you were working for the Lord rather than for people.

Colossians 3:17, 23

✿ Three bricklayers were hired to help build St. Paul's Cathedral in London. A curious bystander approached them and asked what they were doing. The first bricklayer responded, "I'm laying bricks—I'm making money!" The second bricklayer said, "I'm laying bricks—I'm a third-generation bricklayer." The third bricklayer stepped back, looked up, and responded, "I'm assisting Sir Christopher Wren in building a great cathedral!" When we moms feel the drudgery of changing diapers or chauffeuring kids across town, oh, that we could step back and say, "I'm assisting God in raising my child to be a future leader!"

God's Helpers

GOD'S TRUTH

Then Elkanah returned home to Ramah without Samuel.
And the boy served the LORD by assisting Eli the priest. . . .
But Samuel, though he was only a boy, served the LORD. He
wore a linen garment like that of a priest. *1 Samuel 2:11, 18*

Our children will also serve him. *Psalm 22:30*

The Bible tells us that Samuel was Eli's helper. Since
Samuel obeyed God, he was God's helper too. When little
Samuel assisted Eli the priest by opening the Temple doors
each morning, he was serving God. Children who want
to please God can be his helpers—even in small things.
Choosing to be God's helper brings dignity to every job,
no matter what the size of the person or the task.

PRAYER

Father, thank you for giving us and our children the opportunity to help you through our obedience. Amen.

Getting Rid of Clutter

GOD'S GUIDANCE

You have stripped off your old sinful nature. . . . Put on your new nature, and be renewed as you learn to know your Creator and become like him. *Colossians 3:9-10*

Remove your dark deeds like dirty clothes, and put on the shining armor of right living. *Romans 13:12*

❀ In my house, clutter tends to accumulate as the result of unmade decisions. Sometimes I set papers on my dining-room table, thinking, *I'll attend to them tonight.* But five days later, the papers are still there. I've noticed a similar pattern with clutter in my heart. If I dwell on how someone has hurt me, instead of dealing with it and letting it go, I give bitterness an opportunity to grow. God's Word reminds us that we need to get rid of the "clutter" of our sin, too. When we do that, our lives will become more attractive as we become more like Jesus!

Help Comes from God

Some nations boast of their chariots and horses, but we boast in the name of the LORD our God. *Psalm 20:7*

He may have a great army, but they are merely men. We have the LORD our God to help us and to fight our battles for us! *2 Chronicles 32:8*

❀ Three thousand years ago, chariots and horses provided military security. Nowadays, we count on stealth bombers and submarines to do the job. God doesn't want us putting confidence in *things,* though, whether they are weapons, wealth, or widgets. Moms may not face chariots and horses each day, but we do face challenges with toddlers and teens. God wants us to look to him in our challenges, trusting him to give us the help and security we so desperately need. What kind of help will you ask him for today?

God Offers Forgiveness

GOD'S ASSURANCE

LORD, if you kept a record of our sins, who, O Lord, could ever survive? But you offer forgiveness, that we might learn to fear you. *Psalm 130:3-4*

He has removed our sins as far from us as the east is from the west. *Psalm 103:12*

❀ The story is told in Spain of a father who began a search for his rebellious runaway teenager by putting an ad in the newspaper. It read: "Dear Paco, meet me in front of the newspaper office at noon. All is forgiven. I love you. Your father." The next day, eight hundred Pacos showed up, all seeking forgiveness and love from their fathers. We, too, need to receive forgiveness. But the beauty of Christ's forgiveness is that if we confess our sin and trust in him, we can receive it anytime and anywhere.

God Holds Us Safe

GOD'S COMFORT

You hold me safe beyond the reach of my enemies.

Psalm 18:48

Holy Father, . . . now protect [the believers] by the power of your name so that they will be united just as we are. . . . I'm not asking you to take them out of the world, but to keep them safe from the evil one. *John 17:11, 15*

❀ We worry that newborns might not get enough to eat, that toddlers might run into the street and get hit by a car, or that teenagers might run into someone or something while they're *driving* a car. Jesus expressed concerns for his children too. He prayed on our behalf, asking God to keep us safe from the evil one. He also asked God to protect us by the power of his name. We can join him in praying these things for *our* children!

Live with Flavor!

GOD'S DIRECTION

You are the salt of the earth. But what good is salt if it has lost its flavor? Can you make it salty again? It will be thrown out and trampled underfoot as worthless. *Matthew 5:13*

Salt is good for seasoning. . . . You must have the qualities of salt among yourselves and live in peace with each other.
Mark 9:50

❁ Yesterday I sprinkled salt into the batter when I was baking Irish soda bread, and later in the day I used it when I prepared lasagna. Salt was an important commodity in Bible times, too. Not only was it used as a seasoning, but it was also used to preserve and purify. When Jesus taught that his believers are the salt of the earth, he was referring to the properties of faithfulness, dependability, and preservation. Just as salt provides these things for our food, Christians exhibit these qualities in the world today. A Christian mom's flavor is tasted first in her home!

God's Purposes Prevail

GOD'S HOPE

The Jewish elders continued their work, and they were greatly encouraged by the preaching of the prophets Haggai and Zechariah son of Iddo. The Temple was finally finished, as had been commanded by the God of Israel and decreed by Cyrus, Darius, and Artaxerxes, the kings of Persia. *Ezra 6:14*

❀ God used *one little paragraph* from a scroll that seemed to have been lost in a pagan library to prompt the completion of his Temple (see Ezra 6:1-5). Is there a good work in your life or your child's life that seems to have been derailed, and you're not quite sure how God will get things moving again? Listen to the uplifting teaching of God's Word—not to the voice of the tempter. If we place our faith in God, he will guide us in paths we might never have imagined.

God Provides

GOD'S PROMISE

"What can I do to help you?" Elisha asked. "Tell me, what do you have in the house?" "Nothing at all, except a flask of olive oil," she replied. *2 Kings 4:2*

God will generously provide all you need. Then you will always have . . . plenty left over to share with others.
2 Corinthians 9:8

✿ "Just a little oil," the widow told the prophet Elisha. "That's all that I have in my house." She had lost her husband, and now she feared that her creditor might come and take away her two sons as slaves. When the widow was feeling totally helpless, Elisha told her to borrow many jars from her neighbors and pour oil into each one. The oil flowed until she and her sons filled the last jar! When the painful realities of life leave us feeling needy, we can run to God. He is still the God who sees and provides.

Wisdom Is Found in God

GOD'S WISDOM

But do people know where to find wisdom? . . . It cannot be bought with gold. . . . God alone understands the way to wisdom . . . and this is what he says to all humanity: "The fear of the Lord is true wisdom; to forsake evil is real understanding." *Job 28:12, 15, 23, 28*

Do you own a piece of gold jewelry? The next time you need wisdom on a parenting issue, let that jewelry remind you that there isn't enough gold in the whole world to purchase an answer to such questions. However, the Bible has encouraging news! We don't need money to find wisdom because wisdom is found in fearing God. That means seeing God for who he is and responding to him with reverent and affectionate obedience.

PRAYER

Father, I look to you for wisdom and help today. Amen.

Completing Our Work

GOD'S CHALLENGE

After Jesus said this, he looked toward heaven and prayed: "Father, the time has come. Glorify your Son, that your Son may glorify you . . . I have brought you glory on earth by completing the work you gave me to do." *John 17:1, 4 NIV*

❀ None of us is perfect, and no mom on earth will ever do a perfect job of mothering. But when we come to the end of our mothering days, we want to feel that we have completed our tasks well. When Jesus was nearing the end of his time on earth, he spoke with confidence about completing God's work. What was that work? Pointing people to God (John 1:18); modeling justice, mercy, and humility (Micah 6:8); making disciples (Matthew 28:19-20); and serving through sacrifice (Philippians 2:5-8). These are good goals for us as well.

PRAYER

Father, please strengthen us to complete our work for you. Amen.

Share What God Has Done

GOD'S TRUTH

I have told all your people about your justice. I have not been afraid to speak out, as you, O LORD, well know. I have not kept the good news of your justice hidden in my heart; I have talked about your faithfulness and saving power. I have told everyone in the great assembly of your unfailing love and faithfulness. *Psalm 40:9-10*

❀ When my children were very young, I chose our pediatrician on the recommendation of other moms I knew. One of the reasons my family moved to the north side of Wheaton was because we heard how great the neighborhood elementary school was. We are often quick to speak to friends and family about doctors, schools, or bargains at the grocery store. Are we as quick to share what God has done for us? How has God shown you his love—his faithfulness? Share it with someone today!

Be Encouraging

GOD'S GUIDANCE

Do not aggravate your children, or they will become discouraged. *Colossians 3:21*

Worry weighs a person down; an encouraging word cheers a person up. *Proverbs 12:25*

❀ The story is told of a teacher who asked her students what they wanted to become when they grew up. "President." "A fireman." "A teacher." One by one they answered. When it was Billy's turn, he said, "Possible." "Possible?" asked the teacher. "Yes," Billy responded. "My mom is always telling me I'm impossible. When I grow up I want to become *possible.*" Our words should build our children up, not tear them down. When I'm looking for help to be an encouraging mom, the verses above are a great place to start!

PRAYER

Father, may I look to you and your Word for help to be an encouraging mom. Amen.

Wait Patiently

GOD'S ENCOURAGEMENT

I waited patiently for the LORD to help me, and he turned to me and heard my cry. He lifted me out of the pit of despair, out of the mud and the mire. He set my feet on solid ground and steadied me as I walked along. *Psalm 40:1-2*

Over the course of our lives, we sometimes experience times of despair. Whether we're feeling gloomy and miserable because of sickness, sin, or loss, it seems as though we've sunk into a deep hole and we're struggling to get out. What do we do? Wait patiently. That may not sound very uplifting, but encouragement comes from seeing the things that *God* does. He helps us, turns to us, hears our cries, lifts us out of the pit of despair, sets our feet on solid ground, and steadies us (Psalm 40:1-2). When we wait patiently for God, he will lift us up.

Growing Close to God

GOD'S ASSURANCE

Because of Christ and our faith in him, we can now come boldly and confidently into God's presence. *Ephesians 3:12*

Therefore, since we have been made right in God's sight by faith, we have peace with God because of what Jesus Christ our Lord has done for us. *Romans 5:1*

✿ Romans 5:1-5 tells us we can receive peace with God, access to God, hope, confidence amid the daily trials of life, and a personal experience with God's love. Money can't buy these things! They are gifts of God's grace that we can receive through faith in Christ. These gifts are available to us any time, even in the midst of our daily routines.

PRAYER

Father, thank you that the privilege of knowing you doesn't depend on money or good deeds, but that it comes through faith in Christ. Amen.

What God Wants

GOD'S DIRECTION

What can we bring to the LORD? . . . Should we offer him
. . . ten thousand rivers of olive oil? . . . No, O people, the
LORD has told you what is good, and this is what he requires
of you: to do what is right, to love mercy, and to walk humbly with your God. *Micah 6:6-8*

❀ Back at the time of the Old Testament prophet Micah,
God said he wasn't looking for sacrifices and religious ritu-
als. He was looking for changed lives, and that's still what
he seeks from us today. We sometimes try to appease God
with church attendance, church activities, and other religious "stuff," but God wants us to *do what is right, love
mercy, and walk humbly with God.* These are simple—not
easy—things that moms can do anytime and anywhere. If
we want to do them, God will help us.

God Can Transform Us

GOD'S HOPE

Don't copy the behavior and customs of this world, but let God transform you into a new person by changing the way you think. Then you will learn to know God's will for you, which is good and pleasing and perfect. *Romans 12:2*

What counts is whether we have been transformed into a new creation. *Galatians 6:15*

※ A plastic surgeon can change the nature, form, or function of our nose, ears, or jaw, but only God can transform our minds. The English word *transform* is based on the word *metamorphosis,* meaning "change from within." Warren Wiersbe says, "If the world controls your thinking, you are a conformer; if Christ controls your thinking, you are a transformer." As we spend time in God's Word, his Holy Spirit changes us from the inside, giving us eternal perspective and a sense of great worth, meaning, and significance.

Four Principles for Life

GOD'S PROMISE

And Solomon, my son, learn to know the God of your ancestors intimately. Worship and serve him with your whole heart and a willing mind. For the LORD sees every heart and knows every plan and thought. If you seek him, you will find him. *1 Chronicles 28:9*

In the last two chapters of 1 Chronicles, David addresses some of his comments to the leaders of Israel, and others to his son, Solomon, who is about to become the new king. The life principles he presents to Solomon are equally appropriate for us to pass down to our children. David uses four verbs that allude to Solomon's responsibility: *know, worship, serve,* and *seek.* Know God intimately. Worship him and serve him with your whole heart and a willing mind. The last principle is full of incredible hope: *If you seek him, you will find him.*

God Wants to Protect Us

GOD'S WISDOM

God's laws are perfect. They protect us, make us wise, and give us joy and light. God's laws are pure, eternal, just. They are more desirable than gold. They are sweeter than honey dripping from a honeycomb. For they warn us away from harm and give success to those who obey them.

Psalm 19:7-11, TLB

✿ Warning our children away from harm and pointing them toward success is what we want to do for them, right? We teach them not to touch the stove or play in the street because we don't want them to get burned or hit by a car. It shouldn't surprise us that God gave us laws for our spiritual well-being. Just as we physically protect our children, God has graciously established laws for our *spiritual* protection. His laws are based on truth and goodness—a sign of his great love and care.

The Windows of Heaven

GOD'S CHALLENGE

"Bring all the tithes into the storehouse so there will be enough food in my Temple. If you do," says the LORD of Heaven's Armies, "I will open the windows of heaven for you. I will pour out a blessing so great you won't have enough room to take it in! Try it! Put me to the test!"

Malachi 3:10

❁ The Old Testament prophet Malachi urged the people of his day not to withhold their tithe—money that supported God's work. He wanted people to catch the excitement of tithing in faith and watch how God provided—instead of thinking of tithing as losing what they had worked hard to earn. One year when I received some unexpected royalties, I sent the tithe to a widowed missionary. She wrote back, "My computer had just broken down when your check arrived!" When we give, God opens the windows of heaven for us!

God Has Power to Help Us

GOD'S TRUTH

By faith Moses, when he had grown up, refused to be known as the son of Pharaoh's daughter. . . . By faith he left Egypt, not fearing the king's anger; he persevered because he saw him who is invisible. *Hebrews 11:24, 27, NIV*

One day a little boy was trying to take the lid off a peanut-butter jar. The little guy was wincing and straining, but he couldn't make the lid budge. His mom smiled and said, "Are you using all your strength?" "Yes, Mommy!" "I don't think you are," his mom replied, "because you haven't asked me to help you! I'm happy to share my strength with you." Sometimes we're like that little boy. We act as though all our strength to persevere must come from us. Remembering God's great power is wonderfully encouraging. We can look to God for help as we persevere with faith.

Looking After Others

GOD'S GUIDANCE

Work at living in peace with everyone, and work at living a holy life, for those who are not holy will not see the Lord. Look after each other so that none of you fails to receive the grace of God. Watch out that no poisonous root of bitterness grows up to trouble you, corrupting many. *Hebrews 12:14-15*

Most moms are good at looking after other people. Although we regularly take care of our families' physical and emotional needs, Hebrews 12:14-15 addresses *spiritual* needs. We can watch out for one another by showing concern about unconfessed sin, lack of love for God's Word, or lack of fellowship among the church body. We must lovingly look out for one another so that we don't miss out on God's grace. As my pastor, Kent Hughes, says, "We all need grace to finish the race." Keep those nurturing impulses flowing!

Trust God for Contentment

GOD'S ENCOURAGEMENT

I know how to live on almost nothing or with everything. I have learned the secret of living in every situation, whether it is with a full stomach or empty, with plenty or little. For I can do everything through Christ, who gives me strength. *Philippians 4:12-13*

Some things in life can be changed, and other things can't—like our families of origin, our genes, or the basic personalities of our children or our husbands. What do we do with situations we'd like to change but can't? Even when we have little control over a circumstance, we can choose the attitude of our hearts. Our contentment will be directly proportional to our trust in God. If we have little trust, we'll find little contentment. If we have great trust, we will have great contentment, because we know God is in control.

Worth the Worry?

GOD'S ASSURANCE

Can all your worries add a single moment to your life? And if worry can't accomplish a little thing like that, what's the use of worrying over bigger things? . . . Seek the Kingdom of God above all else, and he will give you everything you need. *Luke 12:25-26, 31*

✿ "Can all your worries add a single moment to your life?" That's an interesting question! Let's see . . . an average life span is eighty years, so that computes to 42,076,800 minutes. If my worries were able to add one minute to my life—making it 42,076,801 minutes—would they have been productive? Probably not—especially if I ended up with ulcers, which might actually *shorten* my life and would certainly make it less pleasant. Jesus instructs me to trust him, and he promises that if I do, he will give me everything that I need. Now *that's* productive!

Honor God Today

GOD'S CHALLENGE

Don't let the excitement of youth cause you to forget your Creator. Honor him in your youth before you grow old and say, "Life is not pleasant anymore." *Ecclesiastes 12:1*

You are worthy, O Lord our God, to receive glory and honor and power. *Revelation 4:11*

❁ I am indebted to my parents, who helped me to use my time wisely and build healthy disciplines into my life. As an adult, I'm no longer accountable to my parents for how I use my time, but I am accountable to God. And although I don't have the youth of my childhood, I don't yet have the limitations mentioned in Ecclesiastes 12:2-5 of dim eyes, trembling limbs, loss of teeth, or deafness to music. So, if God wills, I still have time to remember my Creator and honor him throughout the 86,400 seconds of each day I have left!

God Never Wears Out

GOD'S TRUTH

Long ago you laid the foundation of the earth and made the heavens with your hands. They will perish, but you will remain forever; they will wear out like old clothing. You will change them like a garment and discard them. But you are always the same; you will live forever. *Psalm 102:25-27*

❁ If your children are old enough, you've probably discovered that they get attached to certain pieces of clothing. Maybe it's a comfy sweatshirt or a pair of jeans. I've put many a patch over holes or tears in favorite blue jeans that—in my opinion—should have been tossed into the trash. The Bible tells us that, unlike garments that wear out, God is always the same. He will last *forever!* Analogies like these remind us that God alone is worthy of our trust.

A Caring Shepherd

GOD'S ENCOURAGEMENT

I am the good shepherd. The good shepherd sacrifices his
life for the sheep. *John 10:11*

Jesus saw the huge crowd as he stepped from the boat, and
he had compassion on them because they were like sheep
without a shepherd. *Mark 6:34*

✿ Throughout the Bible, God is described as the Good
Shepherd, and people are sometimes likened to sheep. The
lot in life of any one sheep depended on the shepherd who
cared for it. A shepherd could be kind, thoughtful, and wise,
or he could be mean, inconsiderate, and irresponsible.
When we see God as our shepherd, we realize that we have
the very best care available. Our shepherd is all-powerful
and all-knowing. He never sleeps, and he cares about us
individually because he gave us life and sustains us. How
comforting! God is our Shepherd.

Turn to God

God's Guidance

"Now my soul is deeply troubled. Should I pray, 'Father, save me from this hour?' But this is the very reason I came! Father, bring glory to your name." Then a voice spoke from heaven, saying, "I have already brought glory to my name, and I will do so again." *John 12:27-28*

Where do we turn when our hearts are troubled about a concern with our children, our husbands, or ourselves? It's easy for a mom to withdraw and feel isolated, mistakenly assuming that she is alone in her woes. But I find it immensely reassuring that Jesus, of all people, spoke about his troubled heart. In a moment of agony and dread, he was honest about his feelings, and he turned directly to God with his questions. He didn't stop there. He also obeyed. Feelings . . . questions . . . obedience. That's a great pattern for moms to follow.

Spiritual Growth

GOD'S TRUTH

I pray for you constantly, asking God, the glorious Father of our Lord Jesus Christ, to give you spiritual wisdom and insight so that you might grow in your knowledge of God.

Ephesians 1:16-17

Some years ago, we purchased two hamsters for our son Jordan. I was not consumed with the little critters like he was, so when I looked at them two weeks after he brought them home, I was amazed to see how much they had grown. My son hadn't noticed their growth, though, because he played with them each day. Spiritual growth happens over time, too. It cannot be forced. But if the elements of God's truth (his Word), God's grace (his body, the church), and time are present, God produces growth.

PRAYER

Father, thank you that as seeds of your truth and grace are scattered in our hearts over time, we will grow. Amen.

More Than Enough

GOD'S PROMISE

So Boaz took Ruth into his home, and she became his wife. When he slept with her, the LORD enabled her to become pregnant, and she gave birth to a son. Then the women of the town said to Naomi, "Praise the LORD, who has now provided a redeemer for your family! May this child be famous in Israel." *Ruth 4:13-14*

❀ It's not hard to think of God as all-powerful and a source of blessing on sunny days when our kids are doing well. What about the gloomy days, though? Ruth, whose story is told in the Old Testament, lost her husband, her father-in-law, and her country. But eventually, God blessed Ruth with another husband and gave them a son who became the grandfather of King David! I'm thankful for accounts of people who dealt with difficult circumstances and found God's mighty power to be more than enough!

Family Resemblance

GOD'S CHALLENGE

So now I am giving you a new commandment: Love each other. Just as I have loved you, you should love each other. Your love for one another will prove to the world that you are my disciples. *John 13:34-35*

Dear friends, let us continue to love one another, for love comes from God. *1 John 4:7*

✿ My sister Gail mentioned a compliment she'd heard about our extended family. While a woman was working alongside my sister at a local resale shop, she figured out that Gail and I are sisters, and that our sons (whom she also knows) are cousins. "Everybody in your family is so nice!" she said to Gail. Grateful for the compliment, I immediately thought of Jesus' words to his disciples—the way we treat others will show people that we are followers of Christ. How can each of us display Christ's love in our choices and actions today?

Break Down Overwhelming Tasks

GOD'S WISDOM

They should always be available to solve the people's common disputes, but have them bring the major cases to you. Let the leaders decide the smaller matters themselves. They will help you carry the load, making the task easier for you. If you follow this advice, . . . then you will be able to endure the pressures. *Exodus 18:22-23*

✿ Are you facing a challenge, project, or responsibility that looms larger than life? Sometimes we feel paralyzed just *thinking* about such things! Moses' father-in-law, Jethro, had some great advice that's helpful for moms, too. When facing a monumental or overwhelming job, it helps to break it into smaller pieces. And—whenever possible—we should delegate parts of it to our children. It allows them an opportunity to grow in skills God has blessed them with, and it preserves our time!

Humility Is Endearing

GOD'S TRUTH

The LORD supports the humble, but he brings the wicked down into the dust. *Psalm 147:6*

You rescue the humble, but you humiliate the proud.
Psalm 18:27

For those who exalt themselves will be humbled, and those who humble themselves will be exalted. *Luke 18:14*

❀ One of the few times my family watches TV is during the Olympics. We are drawn to various aspects of the Games, but we especially enjoy learning about the athletes. Some seem personable and humble; others appear proud and even arrogant. I'd rather watch the interview of a humble person than a proud person any day. In my home, I'd rather have my child approach me with a humble attitude than a proud attitude. Throughout the Bible, God tells us that humility is endearing—to him and to others.

Faith Like a Mustard Seed

GOD'S ENCOURAGEMENT

"You don't have enough faith," Jesus told them. "I tell you the truth, if you had faith even as small as a mustard seed, you could say to this mountain, 'Move from here to there,' and it would move. Nothing would be impossible."

Matthew 17:20

❀ When Jesus lived on the earth, he taught his disciples spiritual truths by talking about everyday things—including the mustard seed. Here's a life lesson you can teach your kids the next time they squeeze mustard onto a hot dog: Even though its seed is extremely small, the mustard plant can reach a height of fifteen feet. In Matthew 17, Jesus told his disciples that if they had faith as small as a mustard seed, they would do great things for God. Great faith has very small beginnings!

God Cares about Labor and Delivery

GOD'S ASSURANCE

Do you know when the wild goats give birth? Have you watched as deer are born in the wild? Do you know how many months they carry their young? Are you aware of the time of their delivery? They crouch down to give birth to their young and deliver their offspring. *Job 39:1-3*

❀ Before my son Chad's delivery, my amniotic sac broke at midnight, and he was born at 6:50 the next morning. Two weeks overdue, our second son, Nate, came at 10:40 p.m. with only two hours of labor. Jordan presented himself in a breech position at the end of my third pregnancy, so the doctors scheduled his cesarean delivery ahead of time— 8:30 on a Tuesday morning. Hearing God's words to Job (above), I'm awed that no one in the universe can better share excitement over the births and deliveries of our children than God.

Opportunities for Encouragement

GOD'S DIRECTION

Encourage each other and build each other up, just as you
are already doing. *1 Thessalonians 5:11*

Until I get there, focus on reading the Scriptures to the
church, encouraging the believers, and teaching them.
1 Timothy 4:13

❀ When Moses' leadership over the children of Israel was
coming to a close, God asked him to encourage Joshua—
God's choice for a new leader. In God's plan, Moses'
encouragement helped equip Joshua for the task ahead.
That kind of encouragement is still God's plan for our families today. What abundant opportunities we have in our
homes to encourage our husbands and our children! Does
your husband travel? Tuck a few cards in his suitcase—one
for each day he'll be gone. And don't be fooled by age—
even high school boys enjoy getting notes in their lunches!
"Kind words," said Mother Teresa, "can be short and easy
to speak, but their echoes are truly endless."

God Cares for Every Living Thing!

GOD'S COMFORT

O LORD, what a variety of things you have made! In wisdom you have made them all. The earth is full of your creatures. . . . They all depend on you to give them food as they need it. *Psalm 104:24, 27*

The godly care for their animals. *Proverbs 12:10*

❀ "Mom, come quick!" Jordan yelled from the basement one day. Looking into the hamster cage, I realized that one of the threads from the nest had wrapped around the baby's tiny toe, causing it to balloon to the size of the hamster's head. Fortunately, the vet easily took care of the problem. I find it interesting that the God who rescued his children from drowning in the Red Sea and cared for his children like a compassionate mother tells us that we are like him when we are concerned about the welfare of our animals. What a kind God we have!

A Feast to Top All Feasts

GOD'S HOPE

In Jerusalem, the LORD of Heaven's Armies will spread a wonderful feast for all the people of the world. *Isaiah 25:6*

Let us be glad and rejoice, and let us give honor to him. For the time has come for the wedding feast of the Lamb, and his bride has prepared herself. *Revelation 19:7*

❀ I've been to a few scrumptious banquets and feasts in my life. But nothing will compare to the feast that is going to take place at the culmination of human history, when Jesus weds his bride, the church. When we celebrate with other believers from all periods of history and all parts of the globe, any feast we experienced this side of heaven will probably seem like a simple picnic. At that time, every believer's salvation will be fully realized, evil and death will come to an end, and we will see our Savior face-to-face! Hallelujah!

God Keeps His Promises

GOD'S PROMISE

For the word of the LORD holds true, and we can trust everything he does. *Psalm 33:4*

Not a single one of all the good promises the LORD had given to the family of Israel was left unfulfilled; everything he had spoken came true. *Joshua 21:45*

❀ Has anyone ever made a promise to you and then disregarded it? Possibly a child promised to take the garbage out to the street . . . but when the garbage truck arrived, the trash cans were still sitting in your garage. Perhaps a friend or relative borrowed money . . . but didn't pay it back. Maybe a spouse promised to be faithful . . . but wasn't. Isn't it reassuring, then, to read that *all* of God's words are true, and *all* of his promises are fulfilled? God is worthy of our trust. He is a promise-keeping God!

Leading Children to Christ

GOD'S CHALLENGE

You must commit yourselves wholeheartedly to these commands that I am giving you today. Repeat them again and again to your children. Talk about them when you are at home and when you are on the road, when you are going to bed and when you are getting up. *Deuteronomy 6:6-7*

❀ One of my three sons was baptized last night. As I listened to the testimonies of the seven junior and senior high school students who were baptized, I was struck by how many times they said their *mothers* were the ones who introduced them to Jesus. Often it happened at bedtime, when the moms were tucking the children in for the night. Moms are given unusual opportunities throughout the day to share God's truth.

PRAYER

Father, help me to make the most of the opportunities you give me to share your words with my children. Amen.

Self-Discipline Brings Freedom

GOD'S ENCOURAGEMENT

For God has not given us a spirit of fear and timidity, but of power, love, and self-discipline. *2 Timothy 1:7*

Bring [your children] up with the discipline and instruction that comes from the Lord. *Ephesians 6:4*

Joyful are those you discipline, LORD, those you teach with your instructions. *Psalm 94:12*

❀ Some people think, *Who needs self-discipline anyway? It's too restrictive! What I want is freedom!* Margaret Henshaw, a distinguished American soprano and voice teacher, was once asked about the key to becoming a master performer and teacher. Her response was, "Nobody likes the word discipline; I hate it myself, but if you don't discipline yourself you're never going to accomplish anything. I think many people confuse freedom and discipline. They are not taught that *freedom is the highest form of discipline.*"* When we—or our children—learn about the freeing gift of self-discipline, we will benefit for the rest of our lives.

*Joan Ames, "Margaret Henshaw," *American Music Teacher* (February/March 1998): 28, emphasis added.

God's Spirit, Private Instructor

GOD'S TRUTH
You sent your good Spirit to instruct them, and you did not stop giving them manna from heaven or water for their thirst. *Nehemiah 9:20*

But I will send you the Advocate—the Spirit of truth. He will come to you from the Father and will testify all about me. *John 15:26*

❀ Although I have authored several books, my formal college education was in the area of piano performance. I continue to teach a few piano students every week, so I am called a piano instructor. To *instruct* is to coach, guide, or train—and I do all of the above. God has sent his Spirit to do the same for me—to live in my heart and guide me as I get to know God and his truth. I'm grateful that he's with me all the time, and not just for one lesson a week!

Love Is Action

GOD'S GUIDANCE

We know what real love is because Jesus gave up his life for us. So we also ought to give up our lives for our brothers and sisters. . . . Dear children, let's not merely say that we love each other; let us show the truth by our actions.

1 John 3:16, 18

❀ Moms are good examples of the principle expressed in these verses, because we often demonstrate love for our families through our actions. We get up in the middle of the night to feed or calm a crying baby. We clean up after a child who has vomited. (My husband used to say, "Please don't ask me to clean that up, or you'll have *two* messes.") We play Candyland six times in one day. We sit through a three-hour baseball game. When you put your head on the pillow tonight, remember the many ways you have shown love through your actions, and thank God for enabling you.

God, Our Refuge

GOD'S ASSURANCE
You are a refuge from the storm and a shelter from the
heat. . . . In that day the people will proclaim, "This is our
God! We trusted in him, and he saved us! This is the LORD,
in whom we trusted. Let us rejoice in the salvation he
brings!" *Isaiah 25:4, 9*

❀ You may be facing a big challenge today. Whether it's a
decision about a parent's health care, heartache about a
child's choices, or the sadness of losing a loved one, difficult
situations leave us longing for respite from the pain.
Although ultimate victory and release from the painful realities of the present are certain hopes for Christ-followers,
these won't be completely fulfilled until we get to heaven.
In the meantime, I'm grateful that we can depend on God's
presence in the midst of our challenges.

PRAYER
Father, thank you that you are our refuge and that we can
trust you. Amen.

Road Map for Foreigners

GOD'S DIRECTION

Be good to your servant, that I may live and obey your word. Open my eyes to see the wonderful truths in your instructions. I am only a foreigner in the land. Don't hide your commands from me! . . . Your laws please me; they give me wise advice. *Psalm 119:17-19, 24*

✿ My husband and I and our three sons have all had the privilege of traveling to other countries. Whether we've driven on the autobahn or navigated the waters of the Virgin Islands, one thing we've always needed is a map. As foreigners, how would we get around without one? Christians, too, are considered foreigners on this earth, because our citizenship is in heaven. God has given us a map—his Word—to point out the safe routes and the routes that lead to destruction. His Word is not intended to stifle us, but to help us arrive safely in heaven—with joy!

Our Hope Is in the Lord

GOD'S HOPE

LORD, remind me how brief my time on earth will be. Remind me that my days are numbered—how fleeting my life is. . . . My entire lifetime is just a moment to you. . . . And so, Lord, where do I put my hope? My only hope is in you. *Psalm 39:4-7*

❁ Isn't it interesting how close calls can jar us and get us thinking about what's really important in life? Maybe the serious illness of a child reminded us that relationships are so much more valuable than schedules. Maybe being lovingly confronted by a friend helped us see that our lives were out of balance. Psalm 39 reminds us that in the end, the thing that matters most is our hope in God—and how we've been able to influence our children to place *their* hope in God.

The Cross of Christ Brings Peace

GOD'S TRUTH

For God in all his fullness was pleased to live in Christ, and through him God reconciled everything to himself. He made peace with everything in heaven and on earth by means of Christ's blood on the cross. *Colossians 1:19-20*

✻ Recently, I sorted through the contents of a messy drawer and came across something given to me by my oldest son, Chad, when he was six. It consists of several small pieces of notebook paper that Chad had cut, fashioned, and taped into the shape of a cross. On the cross, Chad had drawn a stick figure of Jesus, with nails through his hands and feet—and a smile on his face. I'm thankful that the Cross can have a tremendous impact on us and our children, bringing peace to our hearts through faith in Christ's death and resurrection.

PRAYER

Father, thank you for bringing peace to my life. Amen.

Turn Your Heart toward God

GOD'S GUIDANCE

The eyes of the LORD search the whole earth in order to strengthen those whose hearts are fully committed to him.

2 Chronicles 16:9

That is why the LORD says, "Turn to me now, while there is time. Give me your hearts. Come with fasting, weeping, and mourning." *Joel 2:12*

❀ Heart monitors help cardiologists gain a sense of what's happening inside a patient's heart. In the same way that a heart monitor records data about our physical hearts, God sees clearly into our spiritual hearts. God is not impressed with outward show, but he is looking for people whose hearts are seeking him. Throughout the Bible we're reminded that no one is outside the scope of his love. Even if we've moved away from God, we can turn toward him with a repentant heart, and he will strengthen us!

Comfort and Strength

GOD'S ENCOURAGEMENT

All praise to God, the Father of our Lord Jesus Christ. God is our merciful Father and the source of all comfort.
2 Corinthians 1:3

The LORD gives his people strength. *Psalm 29:11*

As soon as I pray, you answer me; you encourage me by giving me strength. *Psalm 138:3*

❀ My husband and I received an SOS phone call from one of our sons the other night. Driving alone fifteen hours straight to be in a wedding, he was supposed to have been accompanied by another groomsman, but that man's mother had just died. When our son called us, he was hurting. Lonely, tired, and grieving about his friend's loss, our son shed tears—and so did we. My husband and I were unable to be present with our son, but we prayed on the phone that God would comfort and strengthen him. He did! I'm incredibly grateful that we can intercede with God on behalf of our children.

Devoted to God

GOD'S ASSURANCE

Bend down, O LORD, and hear my prayer; answer me, for I need your help. Protect me, for I am devoted to you. Save me, for I serve you and trust you. You are my God. Be merciful to me, O Lord, for I am calling on you constantly.

Psalm 86:1-3

❀ Whatever we give our time and attention to is what we are devoted to. It shouldn't surprise us, then, that the word *addiction* can be defined as "what we devote ourselves to habitually." All around us, we see the hurtful effects of devotion to alcohol, computers, food, and sexual immorality. Psalm 86 offers advice for these addictions! Acknowledging that we need God's help, the psalm's words encourage us to *devote* ourselves to God, *serve* God, and *trust* God—calling on him constantly. I'm thankful that God hears us, answers us, protects us, saves us, and shows us mercy as we devote ourselves to him.

Light and Warmth Forever

GOD'S HOPE

But for you who fear my name, the Sun of Righteousness will rise with healing in his wings. *Malachi 4:2*

And the city has no need of sun or moon, for the glory of God illuminates the city, and the Lamb is its light.
Revelation 21:23

❀ I enjoy living in the Chicago area, but I'm not a big fan of the cold winters. One way I endure them is by planning a trip to Florida in February or March. When I arrive, one of the first things I do is sit in the sun by the beach. The rays of the sunshine have healing warmth! Life has its trying seasons, too, but God assures us that Christ-followers have something to look forward to. Through faith in Christ, we can live with God forever in his eternal warmth and light!

Strengthened by Grace

GOD'S TRUTH
My grace is all you need. My power works best in weakness.
2 Corinthians 12:9

Do not be carried away by all kinds of strange teachings. It is good for our hearts to be strengthened by grace, not by ceremonial foods, which are of no value to those who eat them. *Hebrews 13:9, NIV*

❀ I have read Hebrews 13:9 many times before, but when I read it in my morning devotional time recently, three words jumped out at me—"strengthened by grace." Our hearts need to be strengthened because they are sometimes discouraged, small in faith, and weak. All the way through the Bible, we are taught to look to God for his help and strength, and nothing prompts us to do that more than our neediness.

PRAYER
Father, thanks for strengthening and enlarging our hearts with your unending grace. Amen.

Words That Strengthen

GOD'S GUIDANCE

Kind words are like honey—sweet to the soul and healthy for the body. *Proverbs 16:24*

With their words, the godless destroy their friends.

Proverbs 11:9

Let everything you say be good and helpful, so that your words will be an encouragement to those who hear them.

Ephesians 4:29

❀ When I was in junior high and high school, I studied violin with Perry Crafton, a violinist in the Chicago Symphony Orchestra. During one of my lessons, one of his fellow symphony players stopped by and asked, "So, does she play well?" "She not only plays well, but she has an excellent sense of pitch," Perry responded. As you can imagine, I felt affirmed. Each day, we moms have opportunities to build up our children with encouraging words—words that affirm them and strengthen them. Affirm your children for one character quality each day, and watch them blossom right in front of your eyes!

God Changes Attitudes

GOD'S ENCOURAGEMENT

Then they celebrated the Festival of Unleavened Bread for seven days. There was great joy throughout the land because the LORD had caused the king of Assyria to be favorable to them, so that he helped them to rebuild the Temple of God, the God of Israel. *Ezra 6:22*

✿ After seventy years of captivity, the Israelites had been allowed to return to Jerusalem to rebuild the Temple, but interference began—once again. How discouraged they must have felt. But God intervened! He changed the Assyrian king's attitude toward the Israelites so that the people were able to complete their work. Those are encouraging thoughts for moms when we struggle with our children's outlooks. Even though we can't change a child's attitude, *God can!*

PRAYER

Sovereign God, we praise you for your power to transform attitudes. Amen.

Serving Brings Joy

GOD'S ASSURANCE
Now that you know these things, God will bless you for doing them. *John 13:17*

But if you look carefully into the perfect law that sets you free, and if you do what it says . . . , God will bless you for doing it. *James 1:25*

❀ Some years ago one of my friends died of cancer, leaving three sons who are friends of my sons. Shortly before she died, I asked if there was anything more I could do. She said, "Just keep in touch with my boys." I took her request seriously, and great blessing has been mine. Whether it's been sending cards, praying for the boys, or giving them gifts, the joy I have received is something I will always carry in my heart. We find our greatest joy in obeying Christ by serving others.

Want Beautiful Feet?

GOD'S TRUTH

And how will anyone go and tell them without being sent? That is why the Scriptures say, "How beautiful are the feet of messengers who bring good news!" *Romans 10:15*

How beautiful on the mountains are the feet of the messenger who brings good news, the good news of peace and salvation, the news that the God of Israel reigns! *Isaiah 52:7*

❀ Peace includes the idea of harmony between God and man, healing of the soul, and the blessings of walking with God. When a person brings peace to another, even her *feet* are beautiful! If we want peace for our souls, and if we want to be the bearer of good news for our children and others around us, we must keep our feet on a straight path. How do we do that? We begin by spending time in God's Word.

PRAYER

Lord, I want to be a messenger of good news and peace. Amen.

Meditate on God's Words

GOD'S GUIDANCE

Help me understand the meaning of your commandments, and I will meditate on your wonderful deeds. . . . I honor and love your commands. I meditate on your decrees. . . . Sustain me, and I will be rescued; then I will meditate continually on your decrees. *Psalm 119:27, 48, 117*

❀ Children sometimes need to be reminded to chew their food before swallowing. Not so with cows, who chew their food twice. After food has been partially digested, the bovine brings it back up to chew again—"a cow chewing its cud." This process may seem a little gross, but it helps us understand what it means to *meditate.* When we meditate on God's Word, we bring it back into our minds to think about it deeply. Psalm 119 reminds us that it's good to meditate—or chew—on God's Word!

Heart Mending

GOD'S PROMISE

Then if my people who are called by my name will humble themselves and pray and seek my face and turn from their wicked ways, I will hear from heaven and will forgive their sins and restore their land. *2 Chronicles 7:14*

❀ When something isn't quite right with my child's knee, causing pain and limiting motion, I'm grateful when the doctor can take measures to help the knee function again. Our hearts, too, are often in need of mending. Fortunately, God has given us steps we can take to promote healing! The first thing God asks us to do is to humble ourselves. The second is to pray. God also asks us to seek his face. Serious seeking prompts us to turn from things that don't please God. As we take these steps God has prescribed, he is faithful to forgive us and mend our hearts.

Finding a Healthy Balance

GOD'S WISDOM

Do you like honey? Don't eat too much, or it will make you sick! . . . It's not good to eat too much honey, and it's not good to seek honors for yourself. *Proverbs 25:16, 27*

❀ My mom used to drizzle honey over hot biscuits she baked for us on cold winter mornings. Honey makes things taste good, but too much of it isn't a good thing. Just ask Winnie the Pooh about that! When moms across the country read Winnie the Pooh stories out loud, recounting Pooh's eating a whole pot of honey and promptly getting stuck in a doorway, even children get the idea that although honey is good, too much honey is not. The Bible uses honey to teach us about perspective and moderation, not just in regard to food. We need a healthy perspective for all of life.

God Shows Us How to Love

GOD'S CHALLENGE
This is my commandment: Love each other in the same way
I have loved you. There is no greater love than to lay down
one's life for one's friends. *John 15:12-13*

Just as I have loved you, you should love each other.
                                          John 13:34

❀ How do we understand love, and how do we measure it?
With eight words: "in the same way I have loved you." Jesus
laid down his life for us (John 15:13). To love another person,
we may need to forfeit something valuable to us for his or her
sake. Jesus *shares his very thoughts with us* (15:15). His example inspires us to continue to commune with a husband who
has disappointed us, or a child who has disobeyed us. Jesus
took initiative and reached out to his disciples. Our families will
remember us most for how we cared for them.

What Forgiveness Looks Like

GOD'S TRUTH

He couldn't pay, so his master ordered that he be sold—along with his wife, his children, and everything he owned—to pay the debt. But the man fell down before his master and begged him, "Please, be patient with me, and I will pay it all." Then his master was filled with pity for him, and he released him and forgave his debt. *Matthew 18:25-27*

When we read Jesus' parable in Matthew 18:21-35, we see the difference between a forgiving person and an unforgiving one. The unforgiving person grabs his debtor by the throat, demands payment, won't wait, arrests the person, and puts him in prison. The forgiving person is filled with pity, releases his debtor, and cancels his debt. The only way I can ever practice this pattern is to look to Christ. He will help me show mercy to others since he has shown mercy to me.

God's Word Helps Us Grow

GOD'S GUIDANCE

Oh, the joys of those who do not follow the advice of the wicked, or stand around with sinners, or join in with mockers. But they delight in the law of the LORD, meditating on it day and night. They are like trees planted along the riverbank, bearing fruit each season. *Psalm 1:1-3*

❀ If we delight in God's Word, we are likened to trees planted by a river that bear fruit and prosper. In other words, we're growing and bringing life to others. Spending time in God's Word is the way we figure out how to follow God. As we meditate throughout the day on what we've read, we're encouraged to apply it to our lives. The more we know and apply the Bible, the more wisdom we'll have to handle the daily decisions of life in general and of motherhood in particular.

Showers of Blessing

GOD'S ENCOURAGEMENT

I will bless my people and their homes around my holy hill. And in the proper season I will send the showers they need. There will be showers of blessing. *Ezekiel 34:26*

Yes, the LORD pours down his blessings. *Psalm 85:12*

From his abundance we have all received one gracious blessing after another. *John 1:16*

❀ When I recently learned a new praise song, I was encouraged by one phrase: "Every blessing you pour out, I'll turn back to praise." *What a great way to praise God,* I thought. When I prepare a meal, I can praise God for providing food for my family. When I watch my neighbor's kids catching fireflies at sundown, I can praise God for his creation. When I read my Bible, I can praise God for seeking a relationship with me. Blessings . . . turned to praise!

Choose Trust

GOD'S ASSURANCE

Job replied to the Lord: . . . "You asked, 'Who is this that
questions my wisdom with such ignorance?' It is I—and I
was talking about things I knew nothing about, things far
too wonderful for me. . . . I had only heard about you
before, but now I have seen you with my own eyes."

Job 42:1-5

❀ Like Job, we're sometimes tempted to excuse ourselves
for not trusting God because we don't understand what he
is doing in our lives. Only God knows the big picture. So
will we doubt him, or will we trust him? I love G. K.
Chesterton's words on this issue: "When belief in God
becomes difficult, the tendency is to turn away from him.
But—in heaven's name—to *what?*" Once we see God with
our own eyes, there is no doubt where we'll turn.

God Rejoices over You

GOD'S COMFORT

The LORD your God is with you, he is mighty to save. He will take great delight in you, he will quiet you with his love, he will rejoice over you with singing. *Zephaniah 3:17*, NIV

Then God will rejoice over you as a bridegroom rejoices over his bride. *Isaiah 62:5*

❀ I enjoyed singing to my children when they were little, even while they were still in my womb. I like to think of God singing over me—not with me or to me, but *over* me. It reminds me of times when my baby was tired and oh-so-fussy. I would lay him down in the crib, gently rub or pat his back or shoulder, and continue singing for as long as it took him to fall asleep. Next time you're struggling to feel loved, revisit this verse and remember that God wants to rejoice over *you* with singing!

Warning!

God's Direction

Dear friends, I warn you as "temporary residents and foreigners" to keep away from worldly desires that wage war
against your very souls. *1 Peter 2:11*

Clothe yourself with the presence of the Lord Jesus Christ.
And don't let yourself think about ways to indulge your evil
desires. *Romans 13:14*

As newlyweds, my husband and I lived in an apartment
right next to the train tracks. One night a freight train
derailed, sending ammonia tankers lurching into the street.
Jim and I woke up to firemen pounding on our door, warning us to evacuate the building, which we did. Everyone
cooperated, and no one was harmed. The Bible warns us
very clearly about something more serious—evil desires that
threaten our souls. As moms, we are wise to take heed and
pass on warnings to our children. We can also clothe ourselves with the presence of Christ—the very best protection.

Reflect Christ's Righteousness

GOD'S HOPE

The way of the righteous is like the first gleam of dawn, which shines ever brighter until the full light of day.

Proverbs 4:18

Yes, Adam's one sin brings condemnation for everyone, but Christ's one act of righteousness brings a right relationship with God and new life for everyone. *Romans 5:18*

❀ Righteousness is holy living that conforms to God's standards. Because God is both the standard and the source of all righteousness, it's impossible for us to attain it on our own. The path to holy living is not hidden, though. It is well defined. Christ secured righteousness for us when he sacrificed his life for our sins. So what's the path to righteousness? Faith in Christ! As we place our trust in Christ, we reflect his righteousness to our families.

PRAYER

Father, thanks for cleansing us and making us holy. Amen.

Children Are a Gift

GOD'S PROMISE

Children are a gift from the LORD; they are a reward from him. Children born to a young man are like arrows in a warrior's hands. How joyful is the man whose quiver is full of them! He will not be put to shame when he confronts his accusers at the city gates. *Psalm 127:3-5*

❀ Years ago, I was introduced to an older pastor at a convention I was attending. "Do you have children?" the pastor asked me. "Yes," I said, "my husband and I have three sons." I've never forgotten his response. "Ah," the pastor said. "You're rich!" He was right. The boys are a gift—an endowment, a bonus, a legacy. They're a reward—a prize, a benefit, and an honor. They also bring great joy, especially when—like arrows—they hit the target of honoring God.

PRAYER

Father, thank you for blessing us with children. Amen.

Created to Do Good Things

GOD'S ASSURANCE

For we are God's masterpiece. He has created us anew in Christ Jesus, so we can do the good things he planned for us long ago. *Ephesians 2:10*

Now may our Lord Jesus Christ himself . . . comfort you and strengthen you in every good thing you do and say.
2 Thessalonians 2:16-17

❀ As a mother, I don't have to search very far to find ways that my life can count for God's work in the world. I prepare meals and pray that God's Word will nourish my children's souls. I do laundry and pray for the purity of my children. I encourage Christian character, praying that God will use my sons to encourage Christian character in their families someday. With God's help, all of our work as moms can be done with his Kingdom in mind.

Desire Jesus

GOD'S CHALLENGE

Jesus replied, "I tell you the truth, you want to be with me because I fed you, not because you understood the miraculous signs. But don't be so concerned about perishable things like food. Spend your energy seeking the eternal life that the Son of Man can give you." *John 6:26-27*

❀ Imagine what it would have been like to be on the hillside when Jesus blessed the five loaves of bread and two fish, multiplying them to feed thousands of hungry people. The miracle was amazing, but the people were so caught up in having their immediate physical needs met that they missed the real significance of the event. They desired the bread more than they desired *Jesus*—something we tend to do too. The Bread of Life, who was born in Bethlehem—the town called "house of bread"—wants to be our spiritual food each day of our lives.

Pleasure in Obedience

GOD'S TRUTH

What is more pleasing to the LORD: your burnt offerings and sacrifices or your obedience to his voice? Listen! Obedience is better than sacrifice, and submission is better than offering the fat of rams. *1 Samuel 15:22*

I take joy in doing your will, my God, for your instructions are written on my heart. *Psalm 40:8*

❀ Few things have given my husband, Jim, and me as much satisfaction as watching our sons do what we asked them to do. Perhaps it was picking up their rooms, taking out the trash, or feeding the cat. What joy to "catch them" obeying. Especially meaningful were the times when they obeyed us out of an attitude of love and devotion. If we moms experience pleasure when we watch our children obey our instructions, imagine how much joy we must bring to God when we choose to obey his Word!

Dealing with Hatred

GOD'S GUIDANCE

Do not nurse hatred in your heart for any of your relatives.
Confront people directly so you will not be held guilty for
their sin. Do not seek revenge or bear a grudge against a fellow Israelite, but love your neighbor as yourself. I am the
LORD. *Leviticus 19:17-18*

❀ As ugly as hatred is, it happens. Even Old Testament
psalmists expressed hatred for some people around them. So
what do *we* do when we feel hatred? Leviticus 19:17-18
offers us help: (1) don't nurse hatred (cultivate, feed, or promote it); (2) confront people directly (challenge them, stand
up to them); (3) do not seek revenge (retaliation), or bear a
grudge (resentment or bitterness); (4) love your neighbor as
yourself.

The four words at the end of this passage are the best
part—*I am the LORD.* With God's help, we can be freed from
hatred!

Our Shepherd Stands Us Upright

GOD'S ENCOURAGEMENT

Why am I discouraged? Why is my heart so sad? I will put my hope in God! I will praise him again—my Savior and my God! *Psalm 42:11*

On that day the LORD their God will rescue his people, just as a shepherd rescues his sheep. *Zechariah 9:16*

A sheep becomes *downcast* when it lies down and its center of gravity shifts so that its feet no longer touch the ground. At this point the sheep, realizing that it can't possibly regain its footing on its own, frequently panics. The only hope for a downcast sheep is the shepherd, who sets it upright. Moms can become downcast too. When we do, hope is found in God, our Shepherd, who can stand *us* upright. He is the One who can help us.

PRAYER

Father, thank you for helping us regain our footing when we become downcast. Amen.

We Can Talk Directly to God

GOD'S ASSURANCE

At that time you won't need to ask me for anything. I tell you the truth, you will ask the Father directly, and he will grant your request because you use my name. You haven't done this before. Ask, using my name, and you will receive, and you will have abundant joy. *John 16:23-24*

✿ Before Jesus' death and resurrection, communication with God could happen only through a priest. But when Jesus died and rose again, making us acceptable to God, he made it possible for us to approach God *directly*. It's amazing to know that when we have concerns about our children, we can speak openly to God about them. And we don't need to go anywhere special to do it! Because of Jesus, we can talk to God whenever and wherever we want to.

Faith Like Rahab's

GOD'S HOPE

Faith is the confidence that what we hope for will actually happen. . . . It was by faith that Rahab the prostitute was not destroyed with the people in her city who refused to obey God. For she had given a friendly welcome to the spies. *Hebrews 11:1, 31*

❀ Have you ever wondered why Rahab—a prostitute—was praised for her faith? When Joshua sent two spies to Jericho, they found safety and lodging at Rahab's home. Rahab was so convinced that the God of Israel was going to destroy her city that she put her hope in the spies and their God, risking death as a traitor. Rahab's faith led her to obey. God doesn't care what our past looks like. He can wash away our sins and give us hearts that love him fully and obediently. He is looking for faith—like Rahab's—that believes God can and will do the impossible.

God's Presence Helps Us

GOD'S PROMISE

God is our refuge and strength, an ever-present help in trouble. Therefore we will not fear, though the earth give way and the mountains fall into the heart of the sea. . . . The LORD Almighty is with us; the God of Jacob is our fortress.

Psalm 46:1-2, 7, NIV

One evening when my husband was traveling, one of my young sons became violently ill with the stomach flu. Feeling lonely and distressed at 2:00 a.m., I called my sister Gail, who lived nearby. Through tears, I said, "Would you please come over? I don't want to be alone." She graciously came, and her presence gave me comfort. All of us encounter difficult experiences that God does not remove from our lives. He promises, though, that he will always be *with us*. God is an ever present help in trouble!

God Invests in Us

GOD'S CHALLENGE
[Jesus] said, "A nobleman was called away to a distant empire to be crowned king and then return. Before he left, he called together ten of his servants and divided among them ten pounds of silver, saying, 'Invest this for me while I am gone.'" *Luke 19:12-13*

❀ The *Dean Witter Guide to Personal Investing* reports that if a thirty-year-old begins investing $150 a month at 10 percent interest, by the time he or she is sixty-five, the investment will have grown to about $574,000. Sounds good! As a mom who follows Christ, I, too, have been given resources to invest in expanding God's Kingdom. God has blessed me with life, breath, energy, time, children, his Word, his church, his Spirit, gifts, meaningful work, and an income. I want God to receive a good return on my work.

PRAYER
Father, please help me to manage your resources well. In Jesus' name, amen.

God's Word Brings Joy

GOD'S TRUTH
I rejoice in your word like one who discovers a great treasure. *Psalm 119:162*

The commandments of the LORD are right, bringing joy to the heart. The commands of the LORD are clear, giving insight for living. *Psalm 19:8*

When I discovered your words, I devoured them. They are my joy and my heart's delight, for I bear your name, O LORD God of Heaven's Armies. *Jeremiah 15:16*

❀ The most joyful times of my life are the early hours of each morning, when I spend time with God and receive encouragement from his Word. The Bible sustains me, comforts me, and buoys me up for all the challenges of being a mom. God's Word cultivates joy!

PRAYER
Lord God, thank you that when we have a relationship with you, your words bring joy to our hearts. Please sustain us through the challenges our families face today. Amen.

Personal Faith in Christ

GOD'S GUIDANCE

And now, just as you accepted Christ Jesus as your Lord, you must continue to follow him. Let your roots grow down into him, and let your lives be built on him. Then your faith will grow strong in the truth you were taught, and you will overflow with thankfulness. *Colossians 2:6-7*

❀ The events surrounding each child's decision to follow Christ will vary. Whether it's a Bible story at bedtime, a backyard Bible club, or the lesson of a Sunday school teacher, the goal is always personal faith in Christ. We want our children to believe not only that Christ is important, but that he is everything! We can encourage this by praying that Christ would draw their hearts to him, and we can also nurture their hearts with God's Word. The most important thing in life is what we believe about Christ.

God Doesn't Change

GOD'S ENCOURAGEMENT

But Moses protested, "If I go to the people of Israel and tell them, 'The God of your ancestors has sent me to you,' they will ask me, 'What is his name?' Then what should I tell them?" God replied to Moses, "I AM WHO I AM. Say this to the people of Israel: I AM has sent me to you."

Exodus 3:13-14

❀ When Moses was taking care of his sheep one day and encountered a burning bush, God spoke to him, asking him to go to Pharaoh and lead the Israelites out of Egypt. To reassure Moses that the Israelites would listen to him, God told Moses his name—the only time in the Bible that God's full name is mentioned. "I AM WHO I AM" shows us that God is the same yesterday, today, and forever. As we face challenges in our families, we, too, can look to the unchanging I AM God.

Sure of Christ's Presence

GOD'S ASSURANCE

And be sure of this: I am with you always, even to the end of the age. *Matthew 28:20*

But when the Father sends the Advocate as my representative—that is, the Holy Spirit—he will teach you everything and will remind you of everything I have told you.

John 14:26

❀ In the first frame of a "Peanuts" comic strip, Lucy attempts to catch a baseball, yelling, "I got it!" Second frame: "At least I *think* I got it." Third frame: The ball hits the ground and Lucy exclaims, "Rats!" Last frame: Lucy says, "Sorry, Manager . . . the older you get, the less sure you become about a lot of things." God's presence is one thing we *can* be sure of. When we place our faith in Christ, God sends his Holy Spirit to live in us and to be his representative—for certain.

God Keeps Me in His Thoughts

GOD'S COMFORT

But may all who search for you be filled with joy and gladness in you. May those who love your salvation repeatedly shout, "The LORD is great!" As for me, since I am poor and needy, let the Lord keep me in his thoughts. You are my helper and my savior. O my God, do not delay.

Psalm 40:16-17

❀ When I am aware that a friend or family member is struggling, that person frequently pops into my mind—reminding me to pray and to show my love in extra ways. It is refreshing, then, to realize that God thinks about me. When I feel particularly poor and needy, that is a comforting image to ponder. I'm also encouraged to know that as I search for God, I will be filled with joy and gladness!

PRAYER

Savior and Helper, thank you for keeping me in your thoughts. Amen.

Attitude Check

GOD'S HOPE

LORD, my heart is not proud; my eyes are not haughty. I don't concern myself with matters too great or too awesome for me to grasp. Instead, I have calmed and quieted myself, like a weaned child who no longer cries for its mother's milk. . . . O Israel, put your hope in the LORD—now and always. *Psalm 131:1-3*

The psalmist highlights three different attitudes in Psalm 131. First, his words caution us against being proud and overvaluing ourselves. Next, he acknowledges that an attitude of humility is what leads to the attitude of contentment. Contentment doesn't always come easily, in the same way that a child who is being weaned from breast or bottle is sometimes cranky for a few days. But all three of these attitudes—avoiding pride, embracing humility, and settling on contentment—are possible through hope and trust in God!

Be My Witnesses

GOD'S TRUTH

You will be my witnesses, telling people about me every-where—in Jerusalem, throughout Judea, in Samaria, and to the ends of the earth. *Acts 1:8*

You killed the author of life, but God raised him from the dead. And we are witnesses of this fact! *Acts 3:15*

❀ I recently learned that a friend's husband was the sole witness to a murder when he was seventeen years old. Unfortunately, while shooting baskets on his driveway, Brian saw a neighbor being chased and shot by her husband. In Acts 3:15, Peter preached that he was a witness of Jesus' murder. But Peter witnessed something even more shock-ing—a resurrection! Faith in the death and resurrection of Jesus allows moms to be God's witnesses. We can share with our children that when we repent and turn to God, our sins can be washed away. We can have a relationship with God.

They're Watching Us!

GOD'S GUIDANCE

[Eliezer prayed,] "I will ask one of [the young women],
'Please give me a drink from your jug.' If she says, 'Yes, have
a drink, and I will water your camels, too!'—let her be the
one you have selected as Isaac's wife. This is how I will
know that you have shown unfailing love to my master."

Genesis 24:14

✿ Eliezer, the trusted servant of Abraham, had been given
the daunting task of finding a suitable wife for Abraham's
son, Isaac. Under strict orders to find a wife from among
Abraham's relatives, Eliezer prayed that when he arrived in
the distant village, God would send a woman who would
not only agree to give *him* a drink but would also offer his
camels a drink. That's exactly what happened! I love the
faith of this servant because we see how much he had
learned about God from watching Abraham. What are our
children learning about God from watching us?

The Best News in the Universe

GOD'S ASSURANCE

Just as everyone dies because we all belong to Adam, everyone who belongs to Christ will be given new life. But there is an order to this resurrection: Christ was raised as the first of the harvest; then all who belong to Christ will be raised when he comes back. *1 Corinthians 15:22-23*

❀ Discussing the time, events, and circumstances surrounding our children's births is usually a fun thing to do. The concept of death, however, doesn't engage us with the same appeal. We feel uncomfortable with it, and we fear it because not one of us knows how or when we will die. Fortunately, the most reassuring news in the universe brings hope to our fears. Jesus—the only person who has experienced death and lived to tell about it—promises eternal life in heaven with God to all who trust in him!

March 30

Discouraged? Overwhelmed?

God's Encouragement

The Lord said to him, "What are you doing here, Elijah?" Elijah replied, "I have zealously served the Lord God Almighty. But the people of Israel have broken their covenant with you, torn down your altars, and killed every one of your prophets. . . ." "Go out and stand before me on the mountain," the Lord told him. *1 Kings 19:9-11*

❁ Elijah, an Old Testament prophet, was upset and frustrated, and seemed to have reached his limit. Sometimes we feel that way too. It's easy to lose sight of God's purposes and focus instead on things that we're losing or giving up. But the more we do that, the more discouraged we become. The good news is that God stands ready to forgive us and help us. As we focus on him, he restores our joy.

Prayer

Father, when we're worn-out, may we keep our eyes on you. Amen.

What Matters Most

GOD'S HOPE

LORD, . . . remind me that my days are numbered—how fleeting my life is. . . . My entire lifetime is just a moment to you. . . . All our busy rushing ends in nothing. . . . Where do I put my hope? My only hope is in you. *Psalm 39:4-7*

✿ The months before and after my friend Marty's death were a sobering and significant time in my life. When I sat next to her bed in the later stages of her cancer, Marty said, "A lot of us went to college, married, found jobs, bought homes, had children, and have since been running them around to all kinds of activities. These are all good things, but in the end it's our relationship with God that matters— that's what we take with us." Marty's thoughtful words were one of the most convincing sermons I've ever heard.

The Foundation of Wisdom

GOD'S WISDOM

Fear of the LORD is the foundation of true wisdom. All who obey his commandments will grow in wisdom.

Psalm 111:10

Fear of the LORD is the foundation of wisdom. Knowledge of the Holy One results in good judgment. *Proverbs 9:10*

❀ When my husband and I take our after-dinner walk each evening, we enjoy watching the progress of new homes that are being built in our neighborhood. The first step is the digging and pouring of a foundation. Because any building is only as substantial as its foundation, a house with beautifully painted walls and ceilings would be a pretty flimsy structure if it didn't have any underpinning. The same is true of a wise life. The degree of true wisdom that moms experience over a lifetime is directly related to our fear of—or respect for—the Lord. The more we look to God, the wiser we'll become.

God's Good News

And then he told them, "Go into all the world and preach the Good News to everyone." *Mark 16:15*

By God's grace and mighty power, I have been given the privilege of serving him by spreading this Good News.
Ephesians 3:7

❁ The gospel of Jesus Christ is the most important thing we can teach our children because it has eternal implications for their souls. What is the Good News? Jesus was born as a man, lived on the earth without sinning, died a terrible death on a cross, and was proven to be the Son of God when God raised him from the dead through the power of the Holy Spirit. God did all this for us—to save us from the penalty of our sin and provide a relationship with him both now and forever. We can thank God for this every day!

Notice, Speak, Provide

GOD'S TRUTH

When Jesus saw his mother standing there beside the disciple he loved, he said to her, "Dear woman, here is your son." And he said to this disciple, "Here is your mother." And from then on this disciple took her into his home.

John 19:26-27

❀ Even when he was dying, Jesus left us an example for our own relationships: He *noticed*, he *spoke*, and he *provided*. In spite of the fact that he had been hanging on the cross for hours and was very near death, he *noticed* his mother and his friend. Even though it took great physical effort, Jesus *spoke* to John and Mary, reminding them of how much he cared. Jesus *provided* for Mary by asking John to take her home with him. Jesus' example of noticing, speaking, and providing is a wonderful pattern for all of our friendships and family relationships.

PRAYER

Lord, thank you for your good example. Help me to notice, speak, and provide for others in my life. Amen.

God's Wardrobe

GOD'S GUIDANCE

Since God chose you to be the holy people he loves, you must clothe yourselves with tenderhearted mercy, kindness, humility, gentleness, and patience. Make allowance for each other's faults, and forgive anyone who offends you. Remember, the Lord forgave you, so you must forgive others. Above all, clothe yourselves with love, which binds us all together in perfect harmony. *Colossians 3:12-14*

❀ Each morning, I choose the clothes I'll wear, put them on, and get on with my day. The clothes I select may not have much effect on how my day goes. But the way I clothe my heart has a big impact on how my *life* goes. If I choose to wear the garments of mercy, kindness, humility, gentleness, and patience, my life will be much different than if I choose the garments of anger, greed, or immorality. Which garments will it be today?

God's Presence and Favor

GOD'S ENCOURAGEMENT

Then Moses said, "If you don't personally go with us, don't make us leave this place. How will anyone know that you look favorably on me—on me and on your people—if you don't go with us? For your presence among us sets your people and me apart from all other people on the earth."

Exodus 33:15-16

❀ When my children were young and woke up frightened in the night, it didn't take the knowledge of a rocket scientist to calm them down. What they wanted was me! They wanted my *presence.* If I sat on the edge of their beds and rubbed their backs, they would calm down and fall asleep. It's encouraging to know that even Moses—a great man of God—felt needy and cried out for God's presence and favor. God responded to Moses, and he will respond to us, too!

Lost and Found

GOD'S ASSURANCE

Jesus told them this story: "If a man has a hundred sheep and one of them gets lost, what will he do? Won't he leave the ninety-nine others in the wilderness and go to search for the one that is lost until he finds it?" *Luke 15:3-4*

✿ I recently left my favorite black cardigan in a rental car. Even though I went back to the rental office within minutes of returning the car at the Fort Lauderdale airport, the attendants were unable to find the sweater. Bummer! I'm thankful that the shepherd in Luke 15 had much better success. There's something amazing about this shepherd who goes searching for one lost sheep. It's even more amazing to think of Jesus searching for us and for our children. He searches because *he wants to forgive us*. What amazing love!

God Is Our Fortress

GOD'S COMFORT

He who fears the LORD has a secure fortress, and for his children it will be a refuge. *Proverbs 14:26, NIV*

The LORD is my rock, my fortress, and my savior; my God is my rock, in whom I find protection. He is my shield, the power that saves me, and my place of safety. *Psalm 18:2*

✿ A fort for our kids is a cozy place where they can play. But a fortress in the military sense is much more substantial—it's a place of strength and security. God tells us that when we respect and acknowledge him, *he* is our fortress. We can experience the strength and security he provides in any location. As we develop our reverence for God, we will find him to be our ultimate security and fortress in life— our refuge wherever we may be.

God's Word Equips Us

GOD'S TRUTH
All Scripture is inspired by God and is useful to teach us what is true and to make us realize what is wrong in our lives. It corrects us when we are wrong and teaches us to do what is right. God uses it to prepare and equip his people to do every good work. *2 Timothy 3:16-17*

❀ When I get ready to clean my house, I round up the vacuum, dust cloth, and cleaning supplies. In order to bake homemade brownies, I get out the mixer, beaters, spatula, measuring cups, and ingredients. To do a job properly, we need the right tools! God has given us his Word as the first tool to equip us for the good work of motherhood. I'm thankful that the Bible shows us how to live and helps us know how to do God's work in the world—beginning in our homes.

Love Serves

GOD'S DIRECTION

And since I, your Lord and Teacher, have washed your feet, you ought to wash each other's feet. I have given you an example to follow. Do as I have done to you. I tell you the truth, slaves are not greater than their master. Nor is the messenger more important than the one who sends the message. *John 13:14-16*

✿ Just before Jesus performed the lowly task of washing the disciples' feet, those same disciples had been arguing about which of them was most important. How ironic that people who thought they were so important were about to behave so poorly in response to Jesus' arrest and crucifixion. Sometimes we are like those disciples—we miss the point because of our self-centeredness. But Jesus died for us, continues to love us, and wants to guide us and encourage us. His patience with us can motivate us to show patient service to our children.

God's Love Seeks Us

GOD'S HOPE

But God showed his great love for us by sending Christ to die for us while we were still sinners. *Romans 5:8*

For God loved the world so much that he gave his one and only Son, so that everyone who believes in him will not perish but have eternal life. *John 3:16*

❀ We talk about seeking God, but we sometimes forget how much he seeks us—constantly. We see his love in the beauty of purple pansies or in the gift of a new baby. But most of all, his love was revealed when Jesus died for us "while we were still sinners." He didn't wait until we were good enough. His loving plan for us and for our children is to *redeem* us—to save us from a state of sinfulness and restore us with honor, worth, and good reputation that are all based on *him!*

Obedience Brings Blessing

GOD'S WISDOM

The LORD was with Jehoshaphat because he followed the example of his father's early years and did not worship the images of Baal. *2 Chronicles 17:3*

As long as [Uzziah] sought guidance from the LORD, God gave him success. *2 Chronicles 26:5*

King Jotham became powerful because he was careful to live in obedience to the LORD his God. *2 Chronicles 27:6*

✽ Jehoshaphat, Uzziah, and Jotham were kings of Judah who ruled between 873 and 731 BC. Although each had his foibles, all three left good legacies *because they determined in their minds to seek God.* That's encouraging. The small choices we make today to obey God, to read his Word, to pray, or to serve our family in Jesus' name make a difference. Day in, day out, they add up to leave the legacy of a mom who determined to seek and obey God!

Cling to God's Word!

And the seeds that fell on the good soil represent honest, good-hearted people who hear God's word, cling to it, and patiently produce a huge harvest. *Luke 8:15*

I cling to your laws. LORD, don't let me be put to shame!
Psalm 119:31

❀ When I hear the word *cling,* I think back to Sundays when I took my toddlers to the church nursery. Most of the time they were happy to be there, but on occasion they would cling to me—hanging on for dear life. A child clinging or holding fast to his or her mother is an apt image of how attached God wants us to be to his Word. He desires for us to cherish it and stick to it like glue. As we do, he assures us that he will make us fruitful, and we will not be put to shame!

Prepare for Thunder

GOD'S TRUTH

Listen carefully to the thunder of God's voice as it rolls from his mouth. It rolls across the heavens, and his lightning flashes in every direction. . . . God's voice is glorious in the thunder. We can't even imagine the greatness of his power.

Job 37:2-3, 5

❀ *Crash! Boom! Bang!* You lie in bed wondering, *How many seconds will it be until the kids come jumping into this bed?* Thunder has a way of getting their attention. Consider preparing your children for the next thunderstorm with these two thoughts: (1) if they count slowly from the time they see the lightning until the time they hear the thunder, they can measure approximately how far away the lightning is (one mile for every five seconds); and (2) the sound of the thunder gives us a clue as to how powerful and glorious God is. We can't even imagine it!

Anger Control

GOD'S GUIDANCE

People with understanding control their anger; a hot temper shows great foolishness. *Proverbs 14:29*

Better to be patient than powerful; better to have self-control than to conquer a city. *Proverbs 16:32*

But the Holy Spirit produces this kind of fruit in our lives: love, joy, peace, patience, kindness, goodness, faithfulness, gentleness, and self-control. *Galatians 5:22-23*

❀ It takes only a second for us to lose perspective or to become impatient, angry, or irritable. Growing in patience, by contrast, takes a long time. Patient people are usually people of understanding. Because they are not looking out only for themselves, they are generally not hasty or impulsive. When pain, difficulty, or annoyance comes into their lives, they are willing to stand back and evaluate the situation with some degree of calm. The more we grow in Christ, the more patient we become, because patience is one of the evidences that God's Spirit is present and working in our lives.

Attitude Adjustment

GOD'S ENCOURAGEMENT

It is good to proclaim your unfailing love in the morning,
your faithfulness in the evening. . . . You thrill me, LORD,
with all you have done for me! I sing for joy because of what
you have done. O LORD, what great works you do! And how
deep are your thoughts. *Psalm 92:2, 4-5*

❀ Feelings can help us identify what's going on inside us
and around us. Feelings can be our enemies, though, if we
"camp out" in them or lose perspective by thinking only of
how we feel. If we get stuck focusing on past failures, present struggles, or things we fear in the future, we might wander into deep weeds. How do we get out? By taking our eyes
off ourselves and setting them squarely on God. As we look
to God's greatness and goodness, his Spirit infuses us with
hope about what he will do in our lives!

Reverence for God Provides Security

GOD'S ASSURANCE

Those who fear the LORD are secure; he will be a refuge for their children. *Proverbs 14:26*

The children of your people will live in security. Their children's children will thrive in your presence. *Psalm 102:28*

The godly walk with integrity; blessed are their children who follow them. *Proverbs 20:7*

❀ Reverence for God brings benefits. The Bible teaches that if a parent fears, or reverences, the Lord, she has a secure spiritual fortress. Her children will experience the refuge and protection of that fortress as well. Even if we did not grow up in a family of faith and security, we can choose, through respecting and honoring God, to have that security for ourselves and for our children. What a privilege we have been given as moms!

Pour Out Our Hearts to God

GOD'S DIRECTION

Pour out your heart like water in the presence of the Lord. Lift up your hands to him for the lives of your children.

Lamentations 2:19, NIV

In my distress I cried out to the LORD; yes, I prayed to my God for help. *Psalm 18:6*

❀ Haven't all of us moms, at some point, become frustrated by the behavior or attitudes of our children, our husbands, or ourselves? Perhaps we can relate to the above verse from Lamentations, which expresses the anguish of the Jewish people over the utter ruin of Jerusalem. Although most of us have not had our homes destroyed, we sometimes experience anguish over a rebellious child, a husband we're concerned about, or an area in which we lack self-control. Pouring our hearts out to God in these situations is the very *best* thing we can do. He hears us!

Obedience

GOD'S TRUTH

We can be sure that we know him if we obey his commandments. If someone claims, "I know God," but doesn't obey God's commandments, that person is a liar and is not living in the truth. *1 John 2:3-4*

✾ Knowing God involves much more than mental knowledge—it is proven by obeying God. We teach our children not to play in the street because we don't want them to be hit by a car. So we say, *many* times, "Don't play in the street." We know that our children hear us, because sometimes they even teach the same lesson to their dolls or stuffed animals! But do they really *know?* It's when they obey us that we're sure they know. It's the same for moms. Living and acting rightly serve as the best evidence to our children that we know God.

Quick As Lightning

GOD'S HOPE

For as the lightning flashes in the east and shines to the west, so it will be when the Son of Man comes.

Matthew 24:27

The Lord himself will come down from heaven with a commanding shout, with the voice of the archangel, and with the trumpet call of God. *1 Thessalonians 4:16*

❀ There's nothing like a rip-roaring flash of lightning to cause us to sit up and say, "WOW!" It strikes quickly because light travels fast. Using a globe and a watch with a second hand, show your child that light travels the equivalent of seven trips around the earth in one second! In the Bible, Jesus assured us that his second coming—like lightning—will be sudden. For the believer in Christ, this is not something to be feared. This is good news. We will be released from sin and suffering to live in glorious freedom with God forever!

Be Refreshed!

GOD'S ASSURANCE

Is anyone thirsty? Come and drink—even if you have no money! Come, take your choice of wine or milk—it's all free! . . . Why pay for food that does you no good? Listen to me, and you will eat what is good. You will enjoy the finest food. *Isaiah 55:1-2*

❀ My family loves to vacation close to water. There is something refreshing about being near it. But water is more than good recreation; it's essential for our bodies. We may be able to live without food for some days, but not without water. That helps explain why Isaiah likened our thirst for water to our soul's thirst for God. In the Gospel of John, Jesus reminds us that he himself is the Living Water. God's Word and God's Son both water our hearts, bringing us life and satisfying us with God himself!

Develop God-Given Skills

GOD'S CHALLENGE

Moses summoned Bezalel and Oholiab and all the others who were specially gifted by the LORD and were eager to get to work. Moses gave them the materials donated by the people of Israel as sacred offerings for the completion of the sanctuary. *Exodus 36:2-3*

✿ Byron Janis, one of the outstanding concert pianists of this century, said: "I believe that anyone who does something well is an artist. I don't care whether they are a shoemaker, a plumber, or a chef. Doing something exceptionally well takes talent and love of what the person does as an artist." God has given each of us varied abilities. It's up to us to discipline ourselves so that those abilities can become skills, and then to offer those skills with willing hearts. As mothers, we also have the opportunity to observe our children's abilities, offering guidance and encouragement for them to develop their God-given skills.

PRAYER

Lord, I want to use my abilities for you! Amen.

God Pays Attention to Our Prayers

GOD'S TRUTH
But God did listen! He paid attention to my prayer.
Psalm 66:19

Make thankfulness your sacrifice to God, and keep the vows you made to the Most High. Then call on me when you are in trouble, and I will rescue you, and you will give me glory.
Psalm 50:14-15

✿ When I was in college, God answered one of my prayers in an unusual way. He provided money (in the form of a paycheck I'd forgotten to cash the previous summer) for me to attend a missions conference. Knowing that God heard my prayer and cared enough to provide was a huge encouragement and prompted me to keep praying. When I experienced his listening and his provision, I wanted to thank and praise him!

PRAYER
Father, thank you that you, an infinite and holy God, listen to us! Amen.

Growth in Faith Takes Time

GOD'S ASSURANCE

Jesus also said, "The Kingdom of God is like a farmer who scatters seed on the ground. Night and day, while he's asleep or awake, the seed sprouts and grows, but he does not understand how it happens." *Mark 4:26-27*

❀ When we plant flowers or vegetables with young children, they often ask, "Why do we have to wait so long for the flowers to come up?" Sometimes we ask the same kinds of questions about faith. Whether we're planting bulbs or growing in faith, we need to follow instructions (God's Word) and wait for God to work. God may be causing our faith to grow even when we can't see any change.

Acknowledge and Remember God

GOD'S TRUTH

After that generation died, another generation grew up who did not acknowledge the LORD or remember the mighty things he had done for Israel. . . . They abandoned the LORD, the God of their ancestors. . . . They went after other gods, worshiping the gods of the people around them.

Judges 2:10, 12

❦ The author of the Old Testament book of Judges cared deeply about the spiritual welfare of his people. He warned the Israelites against abandoning the Lord, and he gave them two important things to do: acknowledge and remember God. Throughout the daily events of life—big or little, happy or sad, mundane or exciting—our homes are one of the most effective places to acknowledge and remember God. We can be encouraged that we have this privilege—even as we think about ways we can accomplish it.

More than Enough

GOD'S ENCOURAGEMENT

Jesus soon saw a huge crowd of people coming to look for him. Turning to Philip, he asked, "Where can we buy bread to feed all these people?" He was testing Philip, for he already knew what he was going to do. *John 6:5-6*

❀ Jesus was sitting on a hill with his disciples when he looked up and saw a large crowd coming. "Where can we buy bread to feed all these people?" he asked Philip. A young boy in the crowd had a lunch of five rolls and two fish. Although the boy's lunch was small, Jesus demonstrated that, offered in faith, it was *more than enough.* Just like Philip, we sometimes end up in challenging situations that look impossible. What difficult situation are you facing? Are you willing to step out in faith to seek God's limitless resources?

Where Do We Run?

GOD'S ASSURANCE

My victory and honor come from God alone. He is my refuge, a rock where no enemy can reach me. O my people, trust in him at all times. Pour out your heart to him, for God is our refuge. *Psalm 62:7-8*

❀ When our children are hurt, sad, or lonely, they often run to us. When we moms are hurt, sad, or lonely, where do *we* run? Whether we are sitting in the car, standing at the sink, or walking outside, we can turn to God anytime we need encouragement.

- "Be merciful to me, O Lord, for I am calling on you constantly" (Psalm 86:3).
- "Those who know your name trust in you, for you, O LORD, do not abandon those who search for you" (Psalm 9:10).
- "Praise the LORD, for he has shown me the wonders of his unfailing love" (Psalm 31:21).

I'm thankful that we can run to God and his Word!

Praise God Constantly

I will praise the LORD at all times. I will constantly speak his praises. *Psalm 34:1*

Yes, you have been with me from birth; from my mother's womb you have cared for me. No wonder I am always praising you! *Psalm 71:6*

Let everything that breathes sing praises to the LORD!
Psalm 150:6

✿ Taking a walk with our children and admiring the daffodils can prompt our praise, whether we offer it at that moment or wait until bedtime to talk to God. My eleven-year-old and I praised God one night when we received happy news of another cousin born into the family. When we praise God, our perspective is renewed. We're reminded of how small we are and how great he is. He is worthy of praise! Which of God's provisions or creations can you and your children praise him for today?

Jesus' Light Can Shine through Us

GOD'S TRUTH

Jesus spoke to the people once more and said, "I am the light of the world. If you follow me, you won't have to walk in darkness, because you will have the light that leads to life." *John 8:12*

God is light, and there is no darkness in him at all.
1 John 1:5

✿ When light can easily pass through a material—a piece of glass, for example—we describe it as *transparent.* Materials—such as waxed paper—that let only some light through are *translucent. Opaque* materials, such as bricks, do not let any light pass through. As Christian moms, we want to be transparent. If we follow Jesus closely, his light will lift the fog and darkness, helping us to see our way clearly. His light will also shine through with brightness and color to those around us.

PRAYER

Father, may we reflect your light to our families. Amen.

Testing Develops Perseverance

GOD'S ENCOURAGEMENT

Consider it pure joy, my brothers, whenever you face trials of many kinds, because you know that the testing of your faith develops perseverance. Perseverance must finish its work so that you may be mature and complete, not lacking anything. *James 1:2-4,* NIV

❀ During my college days at Moody Bible Institute, some of my friends played a joke on me. They removed *everything* from my dorm room—furniture and all—except for one Bible passage on the wall, concluding with, "Perseverance must finish its work so that you may be mature and complete, not lacking anything" (James 1:4). Although that incident was not a serious trial, it was a character-building experience. Some trials in life do leave us reeling from loss, though. When they come, we can choose to cry out to God for his strength and wisdom, experiencing significant growth in Christian character as a result.

PRAYER

Lord, please give me the grace to view my trials as opportunities to grow. Amen.

God Is Ready to Help

GOD'S ASSURANCE

O LORD, you are so good, so ready to forgive, so full of unfailing love for all who ask for your help. Listen closely to my prayer, O LORD; hear my urgent cry. I will call to you whenever I'm in trouble, and you will answer me.

Psalm 86:5-7

❀ Now that I'm in my early fifties, two of my three sons live on their own. Sometimes they get very busy, and my husband and I don't hear from them for a while. We have noticed, though, that whenever our sons need encouragement, help, money, or advice, they're sure to call! Then we smile, feeling thankful that they want to communicate with us. Psalm 86 reminds us that our heavenly Father wants to hear from us too. I'm thankful that he loves us, forgives us, and stands ready to help us!

Jesus Is the Name above All Names

God's Promise

Therefore, God elevated [Christ] to the place of highest honor and gave him the name above all other names, that at the name of Jesus every knee should bow, in heaven and on earth and under the earth, and every tongue confess that Jesus Christ is Lord, to the glory of God the Father.

Philippians 2:9-11

I once received a Mother's Day card from my ten-year-old son, Nate, signed, "Love, Nathan—gift of God." I smiled, thankful that Nate was affirmed by the meaning of his name. Our children learn many names in their lifetimes, beginning with *Mama* and *Dada,* but we pray that the name above all names in their vocabularies will be the wonderful name of *Jesus.*

Prayer

Father, you've told us that someday every knee will bow to Jesus. We love him and are grateful to bow to him today. Amen.

God's Word Refreshes Us

GOD'S TRUTH

As the Scriptures say, "People are like grass; their beauty is like a flower in the field. The grass withers and the flower fades. But the word of the Lord remains forever." And that word is the Good News that was preached to you.

1 Peter 1:24-25

✿ One of my piano students handed me a big bunch of pink tulips yesterday. I promptly set the flowers in a vase but then forgot to fill it with water. Several hours later, the flowers had collapsed. *Those flowers* look *the way I sometimes feel on days that I don't spend time with God,* I thought. My spirits tend to wilt and droop. I'm thankful that help is as near as my Bible. There's nothing like a drink from God's Word to perk us up again!

PRAYER

Father, thank you for renewing my life with your Word. Amen.

A Mom's Job Description

GOD'S ENCOURAGEMENT

Her children stand and bless her. Her husband praises her: "There are many virtuous and capable women in the world, but you surpass them all!" . . . Reward her for all she has done. Let her deeds publicly declare her praise.

Proverbs 31:28-29, 31

❀ What might a job description for a mom look like? Wanted: A creative and patient woman to be a cook, chaplain, good listener, fashion consultant, decorator, recreation expert, teacher, chauffeur, psychologist, nurse, artist, gardener, economist, communication advisor, entertainer, purchasing agent, lawyer, and accountant. No pay, but excellent benefits! Another job description of a mom is found in Proverbs 31, where we are encouraged to be merciful to the poor, observant, trustworthy, helpful, energetic, reverent toward God, wise, and dignified. Don't be intimidated by this standard, moms; be inspired! With God's help, we can each be a treasure to our families.

Point to Jesus

GOD'S CHALLENGE

You see, we don't go around preaching about ourselves. We preach that Jesus Christ is Lord. . . . For God, who said, "Let there be light in the darkness," has made this light shine in our hearts so we could know the glory of God that is seen in the face of Jesus Christ. *2 Corinthians 4:5-6*

Over the years, we moms use our hands to point out many things to our children. While reading a book to a toddler, we point to a cow, asking, "What's that?" While baking chocolate chip cookies with a five-year-old, we point to the recipe. Of all the things moms point their children to, the most important thing is Christ. We point them to the Light of the World. We point them to the Savior. Nothing compares with the privilege of pointing our children to Jesus.

God Will Turn Our Tears to Joy

GOD'S TRUTH

Many of the older priests, Levites, and other leaders who had seen the first Temple wept aloud when they saw the new Temple's foundation. The others, however, were shouting for joy. The joyful shouting and weeping mingled together in a loud noise that could be heard far in the distance. *Ezra 3:12-13*

❀ Although there's a vast difference between loud weeping and shouts of joy, those contrasting emotions can often be felt by individuals who are experiencing the same event at the same time. I rejoice on Mother's Day because I have children, but my friend who suffered a miscarriage might weep. This side of heaven, our lives will always contain some times of joy and some times of weeping. We can thank God that when we get to heaven we will experience only joy!

Heartfelt Devotion

GOD'S GUIDANCE

You take no delight in sacrifices or offerings. Now that you have made me listen, I finally understand—you don't require burnt offerings or sin offerings. Then I said, "Look, I have come. As is written about me in the Scriptures: I take joy in doing your will, my God, for your instructions are written on my heart." *Psalm 40:6-8*

❀ Most of us would prefer to have our children show us love and devotion throughout the year than to neglect us but give us a diamond bracelet for Mother's Day. God, our heavenly Father, says much the same thing. He desires that we show him love, devotion, and obedience from our hearts rather than merely obliging him with church attendance, church activities, or money given out of constraint. It is a beautiful thing when we serve God out of heartfelt love and devotion.

Search for God

Those who know your name trust in you, for you, O LORD, do not abandon those who search for you. *Psalm 9:10*

The LORD is good to those who depend on him, to those who search for him. *Lamentations 3:25*

If you look for me wholeheartedly, you will find me.
Jeremiah 29:13

❀ What do you think of when you see the word *search* or *seek?* Hunting for your child's pacifier? Security officials rummaging through your suitcase at the airport? The Bible assures us that if we search for God, certain things will happen: (1) God will not abandon us (Psalm 9:10); (2) we'll be filled with joy and gladness (Psalm 40:16); (3) God will send us encouragement (Psalm 69:32); (4) we will find him (Jeremiah 29:13). If you are seeking God intently, be assured that you will find him!

Mary—a Good Role Model

GOD'S ENCOURAGEMENT

Look! The virgin will conceive a child! She will give birth to a son, and they will call him Immanuel, which means 'God is with us.' *Matthew 1:23*

[Jesus'] mother told the servants, "Do whatever he tells you." *John 2:5*

Mary handled her shifting role as the mother of Christ in an exemplary way. She wrapped him in swaddling clothes as a baby and watched his independence blossom as an adolescent. In Jesus' adult years, Mary witnessed him turn the water into wine at a wedding, stepping back to acknowledge his authority. In addition to being Jesus' mother, Mary was his disciple as well. When we struggle as moms, when we're unsure of our roles, when we need wisdom and help for a particular stage, it is comforting to remember that the One to whom we pray is also One who had a mother!

God Is Faithful and Gracious

GOD'S COMFORT

The LORD must wait for you to come to him so he can show you his love and compassion. For the LORD is a faithful God. Blessed are those who wait for his help. . . . He will be gracious if you ask for help. He will surely respond to the sound of your cries. *Isaiah 30:18-19*

✿ *Gracious:* kind, compassionate, courteous, considerate. *Faithful:* reliable, devoted, trustworthy. Each of these characteristics describes our gracious and faithful God. Are you in need of God's love and compassion today? He is waiting to show them to you if you will approach him. Are you in need of God's help? He will be gracious to you if you wait for him and ask for his assistance. The beautiful promise Isaiah gives us is that God will respond to the sound of our cries. Reach out to him today.

Wash Frequently

GOD'S DIRECTION

Come near to God and he will come near to you. Wash your hands, you sinners, and purify your hearts, you double-minded. *James 4:8, NIV*

Wash me clean from my guilt. Purify me from my sin.

Psalm 51:2

There are some things in the Christian life that only God can do. But there are also things that God asks *us* to do. James 4:8 urges us first to come near to God. Then James asks us to wash our hands—something moms tend to do frequently. Whether we've been feeding oatmeal to a baby or planting tulip bulbs with an older child, our hands come into contact with food and dirt that we want to get rid of. Keeping our souls clean requires frequent washing too. Continually approaching God for forgiveness keeps our hearts soft and allows us to have a closer relationship with him.

Raising Children

[Hannah said,] "I am the woman who was standing here in your presence, praying to the LORD. For this child I prayed, and the LORD has granted me my petition that I made to him. Therefore I have lent him to the LORD. As long as he lives, he is lent to the LORD." *1 Samuel 1:26-28, ESV*

❀ The word *lend* means to give something temporarily, but Hannah was dedicating young Samuel to God for "as long as he lives." That was a long time! Hannah must have had an eternal perspective—both for herself and for her little son. She realized that the time she spent here on the earth was very short compared with all of eternity, and she was willing to entrust her son to God. In the same way, we know risks are inherent in raising children, but we trust our kids to God's eternal purposes and pray for his blessings on their lives.

What Do You Want God to Do for You?

GOD'S HOPE

As Jesus approached Jericho, a blind beggar . . . began
shouting, "Jesus, Son of David, have mercy on me!" . . .
When Jesus heard him, he . . . asked him, "What do you
want me to do for you?" "Lord, . . . I want to see!" And
Jesus said, "All right, receive your sight! Your faith has
healed you." *Luke 18:35, 38-42*

❁ We read in Luke 18 that Jesus asked the blind man,
"What do you want me to do for you?" Sometimes we
worry about a difficult situation for a long time before we
think of speaking to God. In a desperate situation, the blind
man approached Jesus, acknowledged that Jesus was the
Messiah, and placed his faith in him. If you're facing a challenging situation, call out to God in faith. He is ready to
help you.

God Settles Us

Never! Can a mother forget her nursing child? Can she feel no love for the child she has borne? But even if that were possible, I would not forget you! See, I have written your name on the palms of my hands. *Isaiah 49:15-16*

❀ I remember times when my infants were oh-so-fussy— either tired, hungry, or just plain cranky—and the only thing that seemed to settle them was putting them to my breast. A mental picture of a mother who has power to feed and settle a baby gives us a glimpse into the meaning of *El Shaddai*, one of the names of God used in the Old Testament. *El* stands for might or power, and *Shaddai* describes the power of all-bountifulness. *Shaddai* came from the Hebrew word *shad,* meaning "breasted." God is our El Shaddai, the everlasting One who pours himself out for us and gives us security.

God Is Determined to Bless

GOD'S CHALLENGE

I was determined to punish you. . . . But now I am determined to bless. . . . So don't be afraid. But this is what you must do: Tell the truth to each other. Render verdicts in your courts that are just and that lead to peace. Don't scheme against each other. *Zechariah 8:14-17*

Even though all of us come up short in the presence of our holy God, he still desires to bless us. He tells us not to be afraid, and then he reminds us there are things he wants us to do: (1) tell the truth, (2) treat each other with justice, and (3) live together in peace. Whatever challenge you're facing today, be encouraged. God doesn't want you to be afraid, but he does want you to pursue truth, justice, and peace. He is determined to bless you!

Reminders of God's Power

GOD'S TRUTH

He hurls the hail like stones. Who can stand against his freezing cold? Then, at his command, it all melts.

Psalm 147:17-18

Praise the LORD from the earth, . . . fire and hail, snow and clouds, wind and weather that obey him. *Psalm 148:7-8*

❀ My children and I once witnessed a hailstorm so strong that it left the top of a friend's car looking like a Chinese checkerboard. Hail is made up of large frozen raindrops that can be produced during an intense thunderstorm. Liquid water freezes onto falling snowflakes, forming ice pellets that continue to grow as more drops are accumulated. As long as children are inside when it happens, a hailstorm can be a fascinating reminder of God's power in the world he created!

PRAYER

Father, we are awed by your power. Thank you that, although all creation is under your command, you care for the details of our lives. Amen.

Christ's Body Cares

GOD'S GUIDANCE

Just as our bodies have many parts and each part has a special function, so it is with Christ's body. We are many parts of one body, and we all belong to each other. . . . Love each other with genuine affection. *Romans 12:4-5, 10*

Several hours after Jordan crashed on his skateboard and was admitted to Central DuPage Hospital, the senior pastor of our church visited him. In fact, various pastors from the church stopped by for the next five days. Jordan also received about fifty cards, most from our church family. Our church friends prayed and stopped by with delicious meals. One family even loaned us a hospital bed when Jordan came home from the hospital. As a result of their love, we felt a keen sense of belonging to the body of Christ. God's designs for his church are wonderful evidences of his care for us.

Our Hearts Need Tending

GOD'S ENCOURAGEMENT

Plant the good seeds of righteousness, and you will harvest a crop of love. Plow up the hard ground of your hearts, for now is the time to seek the LORD, that he may come and shower righteousness upon you. *Hosea 10:12*

❀ It's spring, and my family is preparing to select and plant flowers. But we remembered that last year's flowers didn't do very well. Was it because of the place we bought them? Did we not water them enough? After discussing the issue with an expert at a local nursery, we've decided that we need to do a better job of preparing the soil. Cultivating our hearts isn't much different. Our hearts need the special attention and tilling of the Holy Spirit, and the planting and fertilizing of God's Word. Then we will harvest a crop of love!

Don't Be Afraid

GOD'S ASSURANCE

"I am God, the God of your father," the voice said [to Jacob]. "Do not be afraid to go down to Egypt, for there I will make your family into a great nation. I will go with you down to Egypt, and I will bring you back again."

Genesis 46:3-4

❀ When Jacob, an Old Testament patriarch, found out that his son Joseph was still alive in Egypt, his heart must have done a few somersaults. Jacob was an old man, so the thought of moving to Egypt was likely a fearful one. But God graciously anticipated Jacob's fears. "I am God," he reminded Jacob, telling him not to be afraid and assuring him of his presence. What a great reminder for any of us who feel frightened today: He is God. We need not be afraid, for he is with us!

Hope Comes through Honesty

GOD'S HOPE

From the depths of despair, O LORD, I call for your help.
Hear my cry, O Lord. Pay attention to my prayer. . . . O
Israel, hope in the LORD; for with the LORD there is unfailing
love. His redemption overflows. *Psalm 130:1-2, 7*

I admire the psalmist for writing with such refreshing
honesty. Admitting my pain to God, to myself, and to others is sometimes difficult, but it is a sign of honesty and
integrity. In his despair, the psalmist acknowledged both his
fear *and* his trust in God. He dealt with his pain in a healthy
way by calling out to God, counting on God for help, and
hoping in God's Word. His pattern is a good guide for
times of anguish in our lives. God did not disappoint the
psalmist, and he won't disappoint us, either.

Trust in God

GOD'S PROMISE

Let's see if your idols can save you when you cry to them for help. . . . But whoever trusts in me will inherit the land and possess my holy mountain. *Isaiah 57:13*

It is better to take refuge in the LORD than to trust in people.
Psalm 118:8

❀ Each of us practices trust each day—probably more than we even realize. When I purchase meat at the grocery store, I have confidence that government officials have inspected the meat and declared it to be free from harmful bacteria. When I take my sapphire ring to be repaired at the jeweler, I trust they won't replace the real gem with something fake. If we find it easy to trust people we don't know with things like meat or jewelry, why would we hesitate to trust the God of all creation with our lives? He is worthy of our trust!

Stand in Awe

GOD'S TRUTH

You formed the mountains by your power and armed yourself with mighty strength. You quieted the raging oceans with their pounding waves and silenced the shouting of the nations. Those who live at the ends of the earth stand in awe of your wonders. *Psalm 65:6-8*

Have your children ever seen a porpoise jump in the ocean or a peacock spread its tail? Through creation, God gives us glimpses of his wonder. I think that's why many of the words we use to describe oceans or mountains—like *majestic* or *mighty*—are words that the Bible uses to describe God. If the mountains and the oceans are *this* glorious, and the Bible tells us that God formed the mountains and quieted the raging oceans, God must be much more awesome than anything we could ever imagine! Next time you see a spectacular sight with your child, thank God for his creation and his majesty.

Remain in Christ

GOD'S CHALLENGE

Remain in me, and I will remain in you. . . . You cannot be fruitful unless you remain in me. Yes, I am the vine; you are the branches. Those who remain in me, and I in them, will produce much fruit. For apart from me you can do nothing.

John 15:4-5

❀ In an essay on humility, Søren Kierkegaard pictures pride as an arrow racing on its course. Suddenly it halts in its flight, perhaps to see how high it has soared above the earth, or how its speed compares to that of another arrow. At that very moment it falls to the ground. If I think too long about how well I'm doing as a mom, I might be in for a surprise too. God wants us to be dependent on him so we stay connected to him. He assures us that if we remain in him, our lives *will* be productive.

Sibling Harmony Is Wonderful

GOD'S GUIDANCE

How wonderful and pleasant it is when brothers live together in harmony! *Psalm 133:1*

You were cleansed from your sins when you obeyed the truth, so now you must show sincere love to each other as brothers and sisters. Love each other deeply with all your heart. *1 Peter 1:22*

❀ Every year, the same two ducks build their nest in the courtyard of my son's high school. My son recently observed the mama duck leading her eight little ducks in a procession. When the last baby duck struggled to climb a step, the other seven ducklings stopped and encouraged him by quacking. When the little duck finally made it up the step, the high school students erupted in loud cheers! As moms, we love to see our children encourage one another too. One result of faith in Christ is showing love to our brothers and sisters.

Is It Ever Right to Hate?

GOD'S TRUTH

The godly hate lies. *Proverbs 13:5*

You love justice and hate evil. *Psalm 45:7*

All who fear the LORD will hate evil. Therefore, I hate pride and arrogance, corruption and perverse speech.

Proverbs 8:13

[The Lord] hates those who love violence. *Psalm 11:5*

❋ I've overheard moms discourage their children from using the word *hate*. Because statements like "I hate you!" are disrespectful to the listener, I'm definitely in favor of putting a stop to the utterances while investigating the feelings behind them. But the Bible tells us that there *are* things that we should hate because God hates them: lies, evil, haughtiness, cheating, violence, and others. Our character is defined by what we love and what we hate.

PRAYER

Father, I want to be like you. Help me to hate what you hate and love what you love. Amen.

The Godly Will Flourish

GOD'S PROMISE

The godly will flourish like palm trees and grow strong like the cedars of Lebanon. For they are transplanted to the LORD's own house. They flourish in the courts of our God. Even in old age they will still produce fruit; they will remain vital and green. *Psalm 92:12-14*

Several years ago, I purchased six perennial plants to use as ground cover in my backyard. Because those plants have spread, this year I transplanted some of the growth to other locations in my yard. All the transplants have been success-ful—in fact, they are flourishing. Moms can flourish, too, even in the midst of change or difficulty. When we place our faith firmly in Christ, he nourishes us so that we will continue to produce fruit and have vitality through all stages of our lives!

PRAYER

Father, we are thankful that faith in you assures us of personal growth and refreshment. Amen.

Practice and Encourage Modesty

GOD'S GUIDANCE

I discovered that a seductive woman is a trap more bitter than death. Her passion is a snare, and her soft hands are chains. Those who are pleasing to God will escape her, but sinners will be caught in her snare. *Ecclesiastes 7:26*

I want women to be modest in their appearance.
1 Timothy 2:9

✤ As the mother of three sons, I've not had the experience of taking a daughter shopping for clothes. Mothers of daughters tell me that the issue of modesty can be challenging. A modest woman chooses to be discreet, decent, and unpretentious. In contrast, a seductive woman chooses to be provocative—hoping to stir up or awaken men's lust. Whether we're choosing clothes for ourselves or helping daughters make choices about theirs, the issue of modesty begins with the intentions of our hearts. Choosing to dress modestly honors God.

An *Ongoing* Friendship

GOD'S ENCOURAGEMENT

For since our friendship with God was restored by the death of his Son while we were still his enemies, we will certainly be saved through the life of his Son. So now we can rejoice in our wonderful new relationship with God because our Lord Jesus Christ has made us friends of God.

Romans 5:10-11

※ Moms who follow Christ have an incredibly rich friendship. As soon as we place our faith in Christ's death and resurrection, we are no longer enemies of God. Instead, we become his friends! Just as a mother draws her baby close to her, God draws us close to him. And what's more, the love that sent Christ to die and the power that raised him from the dead are the same love and power we can call on to help us in any challenge we face today. We are so rich!

God Is with Us

The LORD your God is with you. *Zephaniah 3:17, NIV*

All right then, the Lord himself will give you the sign. Look!
The virgin will conceive a child! She will give birth to a son
and will call him Immanuel (which means "God is with us").
Isaiah 7:14

❀ When I was a new mom, no one could keep me away
from my baby. Even if I took a brief trip to the grocery store
while my husband stayed home with our sleeping son, I was
anxious to shop quickly and get back home. I loved being
with my baby. It shouldn't surprise me, then, that one of
the names for Christ is *Immanuel,* meaning "God is with
us." If we, as imperfect moms, can take so much pleasure in
being with our babies, imagine how much pleasure God
takes in being with us!

Rx for Insecurity: Confidence in God

GOD'S PROMISE

I know the LORD is always with me. I will not be shaken, for he is right beside me. *Psalm 16:8*

It is better to take refuge in the LORD than to trust in people.
Psalm 118:8

Saul, the first king of Israel, was often tossed back and forth between his emotions and his convictions, and he frequently gave in to feelings of insecurity. I wonder if instead of *suffering* from an inferiority complex, he wasn't really *choosing* an inferiority complex. It's easy to be more me-focused than God-focused. We tend to plan and interpret life in terms of ourselves, forgetting that the purpose of our life on earth is to serve God and bring glory to him. "The cure of our insecurity," wrote Betsy Childs, "is not to become more secure in ourselves, but more confident in God."

It's Good to Give Thanks

GOD'S GUIDANCE

It is good to give thanks to the LORD, to sing praises to the Most High. It is good to proclaim your unfailing love in the morning, your faithfulness in the evening. *Psalm 92:1-2*

I always thank my God for you and for the gracious gifts he has given you, now that you belong to Christ Jesus.
1 Corinthians 1:4

There are many ways moms can thank God in prayer, modeling thanks for our children:

- We can thank God for food, breath, strength, light, encouragement, and protection.
- We can give thanks for what God is presently doing in our families.
- We can give thanks in anticipation of what God will yet do.

PRAYER

Father, thanks for being in control even when we feel off balance. Thanks for all you're doing in our lives and in our children's lives. Amen.

Jesus Was Homeless—by Choice

GOD'S TRUTH

As they were walking along, someone said to Jesus, "I will follow you wherever you go." But Jesus replied, "Foxes have dens to live in, and birds have nests, but the Son of Man has no place even to lay his head." He said to another person, "Come, follow me." *Luke 9:57-59*

✿ If Jesus were living on the earth today, he might visit a homeless shelter—to sleep. During the years of his ministry on the earth, Jesus had no permanent home. In other words, the Lord of all Creation submitted himself to dependence on human hospitality. Realizing what Christ gave up out of love for us motivates us to follow him—not for what we'll get out of it, but for the joy of being close to him.

Try It—You'll Like It!

GOD'S PROMISE

Taste and see that the LORD is good. Oh, the joys of those who take refuge in him! *Psalm 34:8*

He satisfies the thirsty and fills the hungry with good things.
Psalm 107:9

He has filled the hungry with good things and sent the rich away with empty hands. *Luke 1:53*

❀ Pediatricians frequently ask moms, "How's your child's appetite?" After all, a child's desire for food is one sign of his or her good physical health. In the same way, our appetite for God is an indication of our spiritual health. Psalm 34:8 is a cordial and gracious invitation for us to "taste and see that the LORD is good." It's as if the Psalmist says to us, "Try it—you'll like it!"

PRAYER

Father, I want to hunger for you! Thank you for filling us with good things when we come to you. Amen.

Thanking God Renews Perspective

GOD'S TRUTH

One day [the serpent] asked the woman, "Did God really say you must not eat the fruit from any of the trees in the garden?" "Of course we may eat fruit from the trees in the garden," the woman replied. "It's only the fruit from the tree in the middle of the garden that we are not allowed to eat." *Genesis 3:1-3*

❀ I read about a builder of upscale homes who said that a key to his success is having a fabulously decorated model home. He wants his customers to walk away feeling dissatisfied with what they already have. When Satan came to Eve in the Garden of Eden, he did not remind her of the wonderful things God had provided for her—he focused on the one restriction. God wants us to come to him with thanks for the things that he has blessed us with. When we do, we quickly gain a renewed perspective.

Praise God Repeatedly

GOD'S CHALLENGE

Let all who fear the LORD repeat: "His faithful love endures forever." *Psalm 118:4*

May all who search for you be filled with joy and gladness in you. May those who love your salvation repeatedly shout, "The LORD is great!" *Psalm 40:16*

❀ "Kids, remember to look out for each other when you ride your bikes to the pool today," I used to say. "Don't worry, Mom," my sons would respond. "You've said that one hundred times!" Do your children ever accuse you of repetition? When I teach piano, my students learn to recognize the *repeat* sign. If it appears at the end of a composition, the student is supposed to play the piece again. Although the repeat sign is a musical symbol, it's a biblical principle, too. Not only does God like to hear our praise once, but he also loves for us to repeat it.

Clean As You Go

GOD'S GUIDANCE

I hate your new moon celebrations and your annual festivals. They are a burden to me. I cannot stand them! . . . Wash yourselves and be clean! Get your sins out of my sight. Give up your evil ways. Learn to do good. Seek justice. Help the oppressed. Defend the cause of orphans. Fight for the rights of widows. *Isaiah 1:14, 16-17*

❀ Part of my life involves trying to keep things clean—the dishes, the kitchen floor, my family's clothes. They are all good things, but sometimes I fear that I spend more time on them than I do on the cleanliness of my heart. Moms tend to "clean as we go," taking care of messes as they arise, and we're wise to approach our hearts the same way. As I confess my sinful thoughts and actions to God throughout the day, he is faithful to clean up my heart!

Sanctification Is a Process

GOD'S ENCOURAGEMENT

May God himself, the God of peace, sanctify you through and through. May your whole spirit, soul and body be kept blameless at the coming of our Lord Jesus Christ. The one who calls you is faithful and he will do it.

I Thessalonians 5:23-24, NIV

❀ When God sanctifies us, he separates us from sin and shares his righteousness with us. The tools he uses are his Word and his Spirit. We cannot purify ourselves, but we do have a responsibility. Our part is to decide—wholeheartedly—that we want to be separated from sin and then present ourselves to God to be cleansed. This process ends only when we get to heaven. But God promises that if we make ourselves available to him, he will be faithful to sanctify us—to make us more like him.

PRAYER

Father, I give all of myself to you—my body, mind, and soul. Amen.

God Is with Us

GOD'S ASSURANCE

The LORD was with Joseph, so he succeeded in everything he did. *Genesis 39:2*

But the LORD was with Joseph in the prison and showed him his faithful love. *Genesis 39:21*

"Soon I will die," Joseph told his brothers, "but God will surely come to help you and lead you." *Genesis 50:24*

✿ Surely Joseph must have struggled for hope when he'd been sold by his brothers to Ishmaelite traders and later dumped in a prison in Egypt. He could easily have given in to hopelessness and despair. But he didn't. Because Joseph trusted in the God who was with him, the God who was faithful to him, and the God who later blessed him with success, at the end of his life he was able to assure his brothers that God would be with them, too. What a marvelous cure for hopelessness!

God Is for Us!

GOD'S COMFORT

What shall we say about such wonderful things as these? If God is for us, who can ever be against us? *Romans 8:31*

The LORD is for me, so I will have no fear. What can mere people do to me? *Psalm 118:6*

❀ On days when we've been impatient with our children or short with our husbands, it's easy to condemn ourselves, perhaps wondering if God condemns us too. But once we have put our faith in Christ's death on the cross for our sins, he doesn't condemn us. He forgives us and he prays for us. God is *for* us!

PRAYER

Father, thank you that at times when we feel condemnation, we can run to you for comfort and confidence. Thank you that your blood shed for us on the cross convinces us that you are for us. Amen.

God Can Use Anything for His Purposes

GOD'S DIRECTION

If you refuse to let [my people] go, I will send a plague of frogs across your entire land. The Nile River will swarm with frogs. *Exodus 8:2-3*

For the Scriptures say that God told Pharaoh, "I have appointed you for the very purpose of displaying my power in you and to spread my fame throughout the earth."

Romans 9:17

❀ In the Bible, God sometimes used animals to carry out his missions—frogs included. Because Pharaoh wouldn't listen to God's instructions to let his people go, God sent ten plagues on the Egyptians, the second of which was frogs. To ancient Egyptians, frogs were symbols of the goddess of life and birth. God, however, used the plague of frogs—and the eventual stinking heaps of *dead* frogs—to demonstrate *his* power.

PRAYER

Father, we're amazed at your far-reaching power. Thank you that you can use all things for your purposes. Amen.

Tuning Our Hearts

GOD'S TRUTH

O LORD, do good to those who are good, whose hearts are in tune with you. *Psalm 125:4*

You look deep within the mind and heart, O righteous God. *Psalm 7:9*

O LORD, you have examined my heart and know everything about me. *Psalm 139:1*

❀ When I began studying the violin, one of the first things I learned was how to tune my instrument. After listening to G, D, A, and E on my pitch pipe, I tightened or loosened the strings of my violin until they were in tune. Learning how to tune my heart to God has been more challenging. The only way I know how is to ask God to examine my heart and make necessary adjustments. He alone is the perfect standard, he knows me best, and only he can transform my heart from the inside out.

Encouragement and Endurance Produce Hope

GOD'S HOPE

For everything that was written in the past was written to teach us, so that through endurance and the encouragement of the Scriptures we might have hope. *Romans 15:4, NIV*

When doubts filled my mind, your comfort gave me renewed hope and cheer. *Psalm 94:19*

✿ A large part of a believer's hope comes from the *encouragement* of God's Word. Sometimes we read it ourselves, other times we hear God's Word taught at church or a Bible study, and hopefully our friends encourage us with it from time to time. *Endurance* is another aspect of hope. We can give our children lots of encouragement on their homework, but unless they choose to *do* it—to endure—they have no hope of excelling. Hope is like that for us too. We receive encouragement from God's Word, and we must also choose to carry on!

Give Worries to God

GOD'S PROMISE

Don't worry about anything; instead, pray about everything. Tell God what you need, and thank him for all he has done. Then you will experience God's peace, which exceeds anything we can understand. His peace will guard your hearts and minds as you live in Christ Jesus. *Philippians 4:6-7*

✿ It's not enough to say to ourselves, *Stop worrying!* Left on our own, we'll come back to our fears. However, God gives us something specific to do when we feel anxious or worried. He tells us to present our requests to him about *everything*. We are to give them over to him in three ways: by talking to God, making a request, and expressing our gratitude. We give him our worries, our requests, and our thanks, and he gives us his peace.

PRAYER

Father, thank you for encouraging us to pray about everything. Amen.

Opportunities to Serve Christ

GOD'S CHALLENGE

Remember him before the door to life's opportunities is closed and the sound of work fades. Now you rise at the first chirping of the birds, but then all their sounds will grow faint. *Ecclesiastes 12:4*

Therefore, whenever we have the opportunity, we should do good to everyone—especially to those in the family of faith.
Galatians 6:10

Opportunity. What a hopeful word! Whether it's a longed-for vacation or a chance to have a meaningful conversation with a child, opportunities often prompt a sense of anticipation. After attending the memorial service of Ken Taylor, the man who paraphrased *The Living Bible*, I came away reminded that each of us has opportunities to serve Christ while we're on this earth. Opportunities to be generous to others. Opportunities to be kind. Opportunities to pray. Opportunities to spend time in God's Word. Opportunities to share the Good News of Christ. What opportunities do we have today to serve Christ?

Prayer Has Powerful Results

GOD'S TRUTH
Confess your sins to each other and pray for each other so that you may be healed. The earnest prayer of a righteous person has great power and produces wonderful results.

James 5:16

We fasted and earnestly prayed that our God would take care of us, and he heard our prayer. *Ezra 8:23*

❀ Here are some practical ways we can pray for our families:

- Pray using Scripture (see Psalm 25:8; 86:11; 119:37; 1 Thessalonians 5:23-24; Hebrews 13:20-21).
- Pray at specific times each day—perhaps during your children's naps or while you're fixing dinner.
- Leave Post-it notes on the mirror or above the kitchen sink to remind yourself of prayer requests.
- Use time alone in the car to pray.

PRAYER
Father, thank you that the Bible promises that praying is powerful and effective. May we be faithful to pray for our families and friends. Amen.

Meet the Author

GOD'S GUIDANCE

Help me understand the meaning of your commandments, and I will meditate on your wonderful deeds. . . . I have chosen to be faithful; I have determined to live by your regulations. . . . I will pursue your commands, for you expand my understanding. *Psalm 119:27, 30, 32*

❀ During some of the literature courses I took back in high school and college, there were times when I had no clue what the author meant. This was especially true with poetry. I found myself wishing that I could have a personal conference with the poet to help me understand what he or she was thinking. That is one of the remarkable things about the Bible. Not only has God given us his truth to follow, but since he's the author, he will also come alongside us and help us understand how his truth fits into real life!

Gift of God

GOD'S ENCOURAGEMENT

For it is by grace you have been saved, through faith—and this not from yourselves, it is the gift of God.

Ephesians 2:8, NIV

Jesus replied, "If you only knew the gift God has for you and who you are speaking to, you would ask me, and I would give you living water." *John 4:10*

❀ I remember a year when my dad shared his bonus from work with all four of his children. He didn't have to, but in his generosity he wanted to. Grace is like that. Grace is the favor and kindness of God shown to us even though we don't deserve it. Grace cannot be purchased or earned because it is a *gift*. Like any gift, it can be appreciated or experienced only after it is accepted. Like any gift, the appropriate response from the person receiving it is "Thank you."

God Cares for Me

GOD'S ASSURANCE

Look at the lilies and how they grow. They don't work or make their clothing, yet Solomon in all his glory was not dressed as beautifully as they are. And if God cares so wonderfully for flowers that are here today and thrown into the fire tomorrow, he will certainly care for you. *Luke 12:27-28*

✿ I love the daylilies in my garden. They're able to grow in just about any type of landscape. Daylilies are part of the plant genus *Hermerocallis,* meaning "beauty" and "day." Although there are many flower buds (up to fifty) on each plant, each orange flower lasts for *only one day.* God assures us that if he takes such good care of flowers that bloom for only one day, he will certainly care for *us* and for our *children* that much more!

Thirsty for God

GOD'S HOPE

I lift my hands to you in prayer. I thirst for you as parched land thirsts for rain. . . . Let me hear of your unfailing love each morning, for I am trusting you. . . . May your gracious Spirit lead me forward on a firm footing. *Psalm 143:6-10*

✿ In the Chicago area, we are presently experiencing a heat wave and a drought. At times, our hearts seem wilted too—we feel the heat and pressure of life's challenges while we are spiritually dry. King David sometimes began his psalms by sharing his discouragement. I appreciate his honesty. He consistently moved out of his tailspins, though, as he remembered God, cried out to God, trusted God, and sought God's guidance. When we do those things, God brings a refreshing drink to our parched hearts.

The Wind That Brings Us New Life

GOD'S ENCOURAGEMENT

But the Holy Spirit produces this kind of fruit in our lives: love, joy, peace, patience, kindness, goodness, faithfulness, gentleness, and self-control. *Galatians 5:22-23*

The wind blows wherever it wants. *John 3:8*

❀ When my three sons tried windsurfing in the ocean, they quickly learned that the sport is much more difficult than it looks. Anyone who steps onto a surfboard with a sail discovers that previous experience with aerodynamics and hydrodynamics is desirable. Just as we cannot predict or control the wind, neither can we predict nor control God's Spirit. But when he controls our lives, we see love, joy, peace, patience, kindness, goodness, faithfulness, gentleness, and self-control.

PRAYER

Father, thank you that your Spirit does powerful work in us even when we can't feel it. Amen.

Stand in Truth

GOD'S CHALLENGE

Stay alert! Watch out for your great enemy, the devil. He prowls around like a roaring lion, looking for someone to devour. Stand firm against him, and be strong in your faith. Remember that your Christian brothers and sisters all over the world are going through the same kind of suffering you are. *1 Peter 5:8-9*

✿ The Bible teaches that Satan is our adversary. He slanders and accuses, and his chief weapons are lies. In order for us to recognize his deceptions, we must know and believe God's truth. We don't resist Satan by running away, but by standing up to him with the Word of God. When Jesus was tempted by the devil (see Matthew 4), he responded to Satan's three temptations with Scripture, not with his divine power. I'm thankful that God's Word has such power for us, too.

God Is Mighty

GOD'S TRUTH

The LORD is King! He is robed in majesty. Indeed, the LORD is robed in majesty and armed with strength. . . . But mightier than the violent raging of the seas, mightier than the breakers on the shore—the LORD above is mightier than these! *Psalm 93:1, 4*

✿ I'll never forget the first time that my husband and I took our three-year-old son, Chad, to see the ocean. As we stood on the Miami shoreline, Chad clutched our hands tightly while he watched the pounding and smashing of the waves. If we were to harness the energy of breaking waves between the Daytona and Melbourne beaches in Florida (eighty miles of coastline), we'd generate about eighty million watts of power per second—enough to run a sizable power plant! The next time you're at the ocean, remember that the same God who is mightier than the breaking waves is mighty enough to help *you!*

What Will *Your* House Be Like?

GOD'S GUIDANCE

No one can lay any foundation other than the one we already have—Jesus Christ. Anyone who builds on that foundation may use a variety of materials—gold, silver, jewels, wood, hay, or straw. But on the judgment day, fire will reveal what kind of work each builder has done.

1 Corinthians 3:11-13

❀ Just for fun, ask your children what kind of dream house they'd like to build if they had unlimited resources. Would it be a cottage by the ocean, a condominium in a high-rise close to cultural events in the city, or a brick mansion out in the country? Explain to your children that all of us who know Christ *will* live in a dream home someday. The choices we make each day will have an influence on the kind of home we have in heaven!

Graduation = Completion

GOD'S ENCOURAGEMENT

So you also are complete through your union with Christ,
who is the head over every ruler and authority.

Colossians 2:10

May you experience the love of Christ. . . . Then you will be
made complete with all the fullness of life and power that
comes from God. *Ephesians 3:19*

✿ My youngest son, Jordan, recently graduated from high
school. He received a diploma stating that he had completed
the specified course of study required to graduate. In a similar way, we are able to enter a relationship with Christ
because of work that's been completed—but we're not the
ones who have done the work! When Christ died on the
cross and rose again, he completed the requirement for us to
have a relationship with God. All we have to do is trust him!
What a wonderful gift.

God Is Not Wearied by Our Requests!

GOD'S ASSURANCE

There was a judge . . . who neither feared God nor cared about people. A widow of that city came to him repeatedly, saying, "Give me justice in this dispute with my enemy." The judge ignored her for a while, but finally he said to himself, ". . . I'm going to see that she gets justice, because she is wearing me out with her constant requests!"

Luke 18:2-5

❀ If a selfish, ungodly judge would grant a defenseless and annoying woman her request, how much more will a God who is full of truth and grace hear and answer the prayers of his children, whom he loves? This parable is not intended to encourage us to weary God with our requests. (We can't.) Rather, we're assured that God is very willing to listen and take care of us!

God's Word Feeds Us

GOD'S HOPE

Is anyone thirsty? Come and drink—even if you have no money! Come, take your choice of wine or milk—it's all free! Why spend your money on food that does not give you strength? Why pay for food that does you no good? Listen to me, and you will eat what is good. You will enjoy the finest food. *Isaiah 55:1-2*

✾ It's presently five o'clock in the morning, and the only sound I hear outside my window is the chirping of baby birds, waiting for their parents to bring some food. When moms spend time with God in his Word, we're a bit like a mother bird searching for food. First, we're fed ourselves, and then we have something to pass on to our children. That's one of the reasons I like getting up early to feed on God's Word myself!

God's Power Is Awesome

GOD'S TRUTH

Who else has held the oceans in his hand? Who has measured off the heavens with his fingers? Who else knows the weight of the earth or has weighed the mountains and hills on a scale? . . . He picks up the whole earth as though it were a grain of sand. *Isaiah 40:12, 15*

❀ If you've ever brushed off a child after he's played in the sandbox, you know how *small* grains of sand are—and how easily they get everywhere. The Bible tells us that to God, the weight of the whole *earth* feels like a grain of sand. That's astounding, considering that scientists estimate the mass of the earth to be 5,972 sextillion tons. If you put that into numerals, it would be 5,972,000,000,000,000,000,000 tons! If God is *that* powerful, then he's surely powerful enough to take care of us and our families.

Weeds Choke Fruitfulness

GOD'S GUIDANCE

Other seeds fell among thorns that grew up and choked out
the tender plants. . . . The seed that fell among the thorns
represents those who hear God's word, but all too quickly
the message is crowded out by the worries of this life and
the lure of wealth, so no fruit is produced.

Matthew 13:7, 22

❀ As I pulled weeds today, I remembered an image Jesus
used while teaching his disciples. He explained that weeds
and thorns in our hearts choke out good things and pose a
threat to righteous, fruitful living. I thought about my own
heart. When I complain, I choke out contentment. When I
worry, I choke out peace. When I judge, I choke out mercy.
When I finished weeding, I offered thanks that through
God's power, we can experience victory over things that
would otherwise choke out his truth.

A Sense of Identity

GOD'S ENCOURAGEMENT

You are a chosen people. You are royal priests, a holy nation, God's very own possession. As a result, you can show others the goodness of God, for he called you out of the darkness into his wonderful light. "Once you had no identity as a people; now you are God's people."

1 Peter 2:9-10

❀ If I asked you to describe your *identity,* how would you respond? Our identity includes our character, personality, distinctiveness, and uniqueness. In 1 Peter 2:9-10, we find a beautiful description of our identity as believers in Christ. Not only has God *chosen* us, but he's asked us to represent him to people around us. It's comforting to know that a believer's value doesn't come from what she achieves, but from being one of God's children. Through Christ, we are royalty!

Salvation Is for Everyone

GOD'S ASSURANCE

For the grace of God has been revealed, bringing salvation to all people. *Titus 2:11*

If you confess with your mouth that Jesus is Lord and believe in your heart that God raised him from the dead, you will be saved. *Romans 10:9*

One day my youngest son and I saw a lifeguard perform the service she was trained to do. The lifeguard blew her whistle, jumped into the water, rescued a little girl, and delivered her to the edge of the pool. Everyone nearby heaved a sigh of relief! That not-so-common rescue reminded me that God's plan for the whole world is salvation. Just as every swimmer in the pool was within sight of a lifeguard, so every person in the world is within sight of God. I am thankful that he allows us to turn to him in saving faith.

Pray Morning, Noon, and Night

GOD'S HOPE

Oh, that I had wings like a dove; then I would . . . fly far away to the quiet of the wilderness. . . . But I will call on God, and the LORD will rescue me. Morning, noon, and night I cry out in my distress, and the LORD hears my voice.

Psalm 55:6-7, 16-17

❀ I doubt there's a mom alive who hasn't occasionally wanted to escape to the quiet of the wilderness. I've certainly had the desire to escape from the noise of a crying infant, the messiness of a toddler's diaper, or the inconsiderate attitude of a teenager. When we feel overwhelmed, it's healthy for us to express those feelings to God—just like the psalmist David did. David, a man who was very close to God's heart, called on God morning, noon, and night—and God hears us anytime, too!

No Greater Joy

GOD'S ENCOURAGEMENT

Some of the traveling teachers recently returned and made me very happy by telling me about your faithfulness and that you are living according to the truth. I could have no greater joy than to hear that my children are following the truth. *3 John 1:3-4*

❀ On the mantel above my fireplace is a double-sided frame. On one side is a picture of my three sons standing in front of the Chicago skyline. On the other side is a calligraphic rendering of 3 John 1:4, "I could have no greater joy than to hear that my children are following the truth." Some moms may perceive that this verse is a present reality in the lives of their children. For others, it might be the longing of their hearts. Either way, this is a great verse to pray for our children (and husbands)—daily!

No More Tears

GOD'S PROMISE

For the Lamb on the throne will be their Shepherd. He will lead them to springs of life-giving water. And God will wipe every tear from their eyes. *Revelation 7:17*

The sound of weeping and crying will be heard . . . no more. *Isaiah 65:19*

❀ When I was a child, getting shampoo in my eyes made me cry. Another cause for tears was getting an injection at the doctor's office. As I've matured, my tears have come as a result of bigger issues like discouragement, grief, or relational pain. Back when I was a child receiving an injection, my mom would say, "Don't worry. It will last only a few seconds!" I sometimes imagine my heavenly Father saying the same thing to me about my tears as an adult: "Don't worry. In comparison to eternity where there will be *no* tears, this will seem like only a second!"

Watch Those Sparks!

GOD'S WISDOM

A quarrelsome person starts fights as easily as hot embers light charcoal or fire lights wood. *Proverbs 26:21*

A hot-tempered person starts fights; a cool-tempered person stops them. *Proverbs 15:18*

People with understanding control their anger; a hot temper shows great foolishness. *Proverbs 14:29*

❀ As a result of sparks from an electrical wire, my brother's backyard deck caught on fire last night. Although my brother wasn't home, his alert neighbor called me, and we enlisted the Wheaton Fire Department to put out the small fire. Fortunately, the damage was minimal. The Bible uses the image of fire to teach us an important truth: All it takes to start a quarrel is the spark of one angry word. This is a challenging area for many moms, so it's encouraging to remember that we can ask God for assistance. When we do, he stands ready to help us exercise self-control in our speech.

Pursue the Real Thing

GOD'S CHALLENGE

"The heavens are shocked at such a thing and shrink back in horror and dismay," says the LORD. "For my people have done two evil things: They have abandoned me—the fountain of living water. And they have dug for themselves cracked cisterns that can hold no water at all!"

Jeremiah 2:12-13

✿ At the breakfast table, you and your children hatch a plan for selling lemonade and cookies. Later, you are horrified that instead of lemonade, they're selling dirty water, and they've replaced the cookies with rocks! In Jeremiah 2, we read that God was shocked when his people abandoned his plan for their salvation. They had forsaken him, the fountain of living water, and proceeded to dig broken water pits that couldn't even hold liquid. God doesn't want us to settle for substitutes. He wants us to pursue him—the real thing. He alone can redeem and refresh us.

Jesus Sweat Blood for *Us*

GOD'S TRUTH

"Father, if you are willing, please take this cup of suffering away from me. Yet I want your will to be done, not mine." . . . [Jesus] prayed more fervently, and he was in such agony of spirit that his sweat fell to the ground like great drops of blood. *Luke 22:42-44*

❀ When we think of sweat, we might think of one-hundred-degree weather or a two-mile run. But the Bible records one of the most extreme cases of sweat—in the Garden of Gethsemane, when Jesus' sweat was like drops of blood. Medical journals document that when a person is under great stress, blood vessels around sweat glands can rupture, pushing blood to the surface and coming out as blood mixed with sweat. Jesus knew that under the weight of the world's sin, he would be forsaken by God and experience hell. Yet Jesus took our sins upon him because he loves us so much!

Restored to Service

GOD'S GUIDANCE

A third time [Jesus] asked him, "Simon son of John, do you love me?" Peter was hurt that Jesus asked the question a third time. He said, "Lord, you know everything. You know that I love you." Jesus said, "Then feed my sheep."

John 21:17

❀ These verses are encouraging for any Christian mom who's wondered, *How can I nurture my children spiritually when I've struggled spiritually myself?* Peter had denied Christ three times. He knew he had failed, and so did Jesus. Now, Jesus approached Peter with the goal of restoration. Jesus wanted to know if Peter was serious about his love for Christ, and he graciously offered Peter a chance to demonstrate his love through service. Like Peter, we moms have sometimes failed Christ. Mercifully, his grace seeks us out and offers us restoration. And when we're restored, joyful service is the natural result of our love.

God's Love
Is beyond Understanding

GOD'S ENCOURAGEMENT

Christ will make his home in your hearts as you trust in him. Your roots will grow down into God's love and keep you strong. And may you have the power to understand, as all God's people should, how wide, how long, how high, and how deep his love is. *Ephesians 3:17-18*

❀ Christ's love is so great that we will never fully understand it, but the shore of a vast ocean is one of the best places to think about the extremes of his love. As far as our eyes can see to the left, to the right, and straight ahead, there is no end in sight. Picturing the extent of God's love is especially helpful on days when we don't feel particularly loved by our husbands or feel like being loving to our children. I'm thankful that God shares *his* love with us.

PRAYER

Father, please fill us with your incredible love. Amen.

God Never Loses Sight of Me

GOD'S ASSURANCE

You know when I sit down or stand up. You know my thoughts even when I'm far away. . . . I can never escape from your Spirit! I can never get away from your presence!

Psalm 139:2, 7

"Can anyone hide from me in a secret place? Am I not everywhere in all the heavens and earth?" says the LORD.

Jeremiah 23:24

❀ Has one of your children ever gotten lost? I once lost my three-year-old son for a short while in a bustling hotel in the middle of Denver, Colorado. Eventually, a kind gentleman found Jordan and stayed with him in the hotel lobby until I connected with them. Jordan was crying and I was crying, because getting lost is a scary thing. How thankful I was to see him! How comforting it is to know that we can *never* be lost from God's eyes.

God Renews and Restores

Create in me a clean heart, O God. Renew a loyal spirit
within me. Do not banish me from your presence, and
don't take your Holy Spirit from me. Restore to me the joy
of your salvation, and make me willing to obey you.

Psalm 51:10-12

❀ Whether it's yelling at our kids, speaking hurtful
words, or losing our tempers, all moms blow it sometimes.
Obviously, the appropriate thing to do is to apologize to
our children, admit that we were wrong, and ask for their
forgiveness. According to Psalm 51, it's also healthy to ask
God to do the following: (1) create in us a clean heart;
(2) renew a loyal spirit within us; (3) restore to us the joy
of your salvation. How comforting it is to know that we can
reconnect with God and reconcile with our kids!

Generosity Spawns Joy!

GOD'S DIRECTION

Yes, you will be enriched in every way so that you can always be generous. And when we take your gifts to those who need them, they will thank God. So two good things will result from this ministry of giving—the needs of the believers in Jerusalem will be met, and they will joyfully express their thanks to God. *2 Corinthians 9:11-12*

❀ Our oldest son, Chad, is preparing to teach high school missionary kids in Vienna, Austria, for two years. When my husband and I realized the amount of support Chad needed to raise—a little over forty-thousand dollars—we gulped. Then we remembered that if God was leading Chad to go to Vienna, he would also provide financial support for him. He has! What's more, God's provisions have prompted the joy that 2 Corinthians 9:12 speaks of. Thanks be to God!

Thirsty? Come and Drink

GOD'S HOPE

On the last day, the climax of the festival, Jesus stood and shouted to the crowds, "Anyone who is thirsty may come to me! Anyone who believes in me may come and drink! For the Scriptures declare, 'Rivers of living water will flow from his heart.'" *John 7:37-38*

❀ As long as I give my New Guinea impatiens plant about one-half gallon of water a day, it's happy. If I miss a day or two of watering, the leaves begin to droop. If I miss more than a couple of days, especially in hot weather, the plant looks as though it's about to die. I, too, have a desperately needy heart that is thirsty for God. I'm thankful that spending time with him—reading his Word and talking to him—renews my heart without fail.

PRAYER

Father, thank you for quenching my thirsty heart. Amen.

There's Security in Integrity

GOD'S PROMISE

People with integrity walk safely, but those who follow crooked paths will slip and fall. *Proverbs 10:9*

To the faithful you show yourself faithful; to those with integrity you show integrity. *2 Samuel 22:26*

I will lead a life of integrity in my own home. *Psalm 101:2*

❀ Relationships thrive on integrity. In a marriage where both husband and wife are people of integrity, there is security. Children who are blessed with parents of character feel secure. If our family of origin modeled integrity, we have been blessed. If not, we have the privilege of choosing a different path and modeling honesty, sincerity, and consistency for the next generation. Spending time in God's Word and opening our hearts to his truth will guide us in our choices to take paths that are straight, not crooked.

PRAYER

Father, I want to be a mom who walks on straight paths. Amen.

Pursue Excellence

GOD'S WISDOM

Listen, for I will speak of excellent things, And from the opening of my lips will come right things; For my mouth will speak truth; Wickedness is an abomination to my lips. All the words of my mouth are with righteousness; Nothing crooked or perverse is in them. They are all plain to him who understands, And right to those who find knowledge.

Proverbs 8:6-9, NKJV

❀ When I attended school as a child, I felt delighted whenever my teacher returned a test or paper with the word *Excellent* written on the top. That affirming word signifies distinction and worth—characteristics every child wants to be recognized for. Here's some great news: Any mom or child who wants to pursue excellence can do it without acing a test or paying any money. A life of excellence is available to us all as we pursue the wisdom of God, revealed in the Bible!

Seek God's Will Daily

GOD'S CHALLENGE

How do you know what your life will be like tomorrow? Your life is like the morning fog—it's here a little while, then it's gone. What you ought to say is, "If the Lord wants us to, we will live and do this or that." *James 4:14-15*

Our lives are so brief that we can't afford to live carelessly or aimlessly. James tells us that the best attitude for a mom who follows Christ is "If the Lord wants us to, we will live and do this or that." Those may be words that we speak to our children, but most important, they need to be lived out in a life that trusts God. We cultivate this kind of life by praying and asking God daily that *his* will be done in our lives.

PRAYER

Father, I know you want what is best for me. Help me to seek your will in everything I do. Amen.

Sharing and Receiving Truth

GOD'S TRUTH

In the end, people appreciate honest criticism far more than flattery. *Proverbs 28:23*

[Love] does not rejoice about injustice but rejoices whenever the truth wins out. *1 Corinthians 13:6*

An honest answer is like a kiss of friendship. *Proverbs 24:26*

✿ "The spot on your neck that you were concerned about looks fine," the dermatologist reported to me this morning, "but there's a small spot on your nose that I think we should treat." I felt relieved that the one spot wasn't a problem, and thankful that the dermatologist caught something I had missed. Isn't that the way it goes in our homes, too? Sometimes we see attitudes in our children or husbands that concern us—things they might have missed—and sometimes they see those things in us. Whether we're *sharing* concerns or *receiving* concerns, we can be thankful when the truth wins out.

Praise Helps Perspective

GOD'S ENCOURAGEMENT

O LORD, what a variety of things you have made! In wisdom you have made them all. The earth is full of your creatures. Here is the ocean, vast and wide, teeming with life of every kind, both large and small. *Psalm 104:24-25*

❀ While sitting by the ocean, I praised God as I watched a sand crab. I also thought about how many other fascinating creatures God has made. From where I was sitting, I could observe sand crabs, jellyfish, and seagulls. But God is omnipresent, able to be everywhere at once, so he can see all the creatures in the world at the same time! When I praise God for how wonderful and big he is, my perspective changes. I'm reminded that if he is big enough to have created and sustained the sand crab in Orange Beach, Alabama, he's big enough to take care of my family.

There's Hope!

GOD'S ASSURANCE

Return to the LORD your God, for he is merciful and compassionate, slow to get angry and filled with unfailing love. He is eager to relent and not punish. . . . The LORD says, "I will give you back what you lost to the swarming locusts."

Joel 2:13, 25

❀ At their worst, locusts can black out the sun and eat any vegetation in sight. They've even been known to eat clothes off a clothesline! The prophet Joel delivered the bad news that sin, like locusts, had caused all kinds of devastation among the people of Israel. We read about that reality in our newspapers and understand it in our lives. Fortunately, Joel brought good news, too: Where there is repentance, there is hope! Repentance restores our relationship with God, who forgives us and gives us new purpose in life.

Humility + Trust + Obedience = Victory

GOD'S HOPE

[The angel] replied, "I am the commander of the LORD's army." At this, Joshua fell with his face to the ground in reverence. "I am at your command," Joshua said. "What do you want your servant to do?" *Joshua 5:14*

✿ Are you up against a situation in your life that feels hopeless? Are you discouraged and tempted to give up? Before Israel's conquest of the walled city of Jericho, Joshua must have felt the same way. But he made several good choices. First, he humbled himself before God and committed to following God's plan. Joshua also took God seriously. God said that he had delivered Jericho, and Joshua believed him. Joshua's reverence for God and faith in him prompted his ultimate obedience. When we humble ourselves, trust God, and obey, we will see God's victory over the enemy in our lives and the lives of those we love.

Heart Covenant Brings Change

GOD'S PROMISE
This is the new covenant I will make with the people of
Israel on that day, says the LORD: I will put my laws in their
minds, and I will write them on their hearts. I will be their
God, and they will be my people. *Hebrews 8:10*

❀ Two caterpillars were crawling across the grass when a
butterfly flew over them. The caterpillars looked up, and
one nudged the other, saying, "You couldn't get me up in
one of those things for a million dollars!" It takes an internal
change before those caterpillars can fly, and that's necessary
for us, too. Changes that could never happen from the outside begin to take place when God's laws are written on our
minds and hearts!

PRAYER
Father, thank you that when we know you through Jesus
Christ, your laws become part of our thinking. Amen.

We Can Depend on God

GOD'S TRUTH
No one is holy like the LORD! There is no one besides you; there is no Rock like our God. *1 Samuel 2:2*

For who is God except the LORD? Who but our God is a solid rock? *2 Samuel 22:32*

He showed you these things so you would know that the LORD is God and there is no other. *Deuteronomy 4:35*

If I want to describe a friend as being highly dependable, I say that she is "rock solid"—like an anchor, a cornerstone, or a mainstay. Although I have been blessed with friends I consider to be "rock solid," the Bible assures me that no one is as solid as God. He is the only One in the universe who is totally dependable. We can be grateful that God provides us with such protection and security.

God's Word Keeps Us Safe

GOD'S GUIDANCE

Those who love your instructions have great peace and do not stumble. *Psalm 119:165*

My child, don't lose sight of common sense and discernment. Hang on to them, for they will refresh your soul. . . . They keep you safe on your way, and your feet will not stumble. *Proverbs 3:21-23*

❀ Stumbling can be painful. I recently attempted taking a shortcut in my church's parking lot by jumping from one level down to another level. Bad idea! I stumbled over a median and went sprawling onto the asphalt on all fours. Fortunately, my injuries were minor—scraped knees and a bruised wrist. I could have resisted the urge to take a shortcut, walked along the sidewalk, and avoided stumbling. In a similar way, when I heed the wisdom and discernment in God's Word, it prevents me from tripping and falling through life. I'm thankful for its guidance.

The Bible Guides Us to Faith

GOD'S ENCOURAGEMENT
And now, just as you accepted Christ Jesus as your Lord,
you must continue to follow him. Let your roots grow down
into him, and let your lives be built on him. Then your
faith will grow strong in the truth you were taught, and you
will overflow with thankfulness. *Colossians 2:6-7*

❀ As Christian moms, we desire to see our children
develop deep roots of belief in Christ. Just as our Christian
life begins and grows through *our* faith in Christ, so their
Christian life begins and grows because of *their* faith in
Christ. Our children's hearts will be nurtured by spending
time in God's Word. Today, ask your child to tell you
about one of his or her favorite Bible stories.

PRAYER
Father, thank you that the Bible provides nourishment for us
and for our children, pointing us to Christ. Amen.

Salvation Is Colorful

GOD'S ASSURANCE

"Come now, let us reason together," says the LORD. "Though your sins are like scarlet, they shall be as white as snow; though they are red as crimson, they shall be like wool." *Isaiah 1:18, NIV*

Purify me from my sins, and I will be clean; wash me, and I will be whiter than snow. *Psalm 51:7*

❀ When I was a child, God's use of color in the Bible helped point me to Christ. A seed was planted when one of my Sunday school teachers demonstrated my need for Christ with a simple song and a wordless book: "My heart was black with sin until the Savior came in. His precious blood, I know, has washed it white as snow. And in his Word I'm told I'll walk the streets of gold. What a wonderful, wonderful day—He washed my sins away." God can use such simple things as color to show us our need for him.

Everlasting Life Can Begin Now

GOD'S HOPE

Since you have been raised to new life with Christ, set your sights on the realities of heaven, where Christ sits in the place of honor at God's right hand. Think about the things of heaven, not the things of earth. For you died to this life, and your real life is hidden with Christ in God.

Colossians 3:1-3

❀ Some people think that the gift of everlasting life begins only when our bodies die. For those who trust Christ as their Savior, though, everlasting life begins *immediately,* yielding a portfolio of riches for both the present and the future: God's truth, the presence of his Spirit, and much more. We don't have to wait for physical death or Jesus' second coming before we experience everlasting life. Our faith in Christ makes it a present reality!

PRAYER

Father, thanks for the present and future promise of eternal life. Amen.

Guard Your Heart

GOD'S CHALLENGE

A good person produces good things from the treasury of a good heart, and an evil person produces evil things from the treasury of an evil heart. What you say flows from what is in your heart. *Luke 6:45*

Above all else, guard your heart, for it is the wellspring of life. *Proverbs 4:23, NIV*

❀ What is a wellspring? It is the source of a stream or a spring, the point where something springs into being, or the place where things are created. What a fitting picture of our hearts, where thoughts, attitudes, and actions are initiated. More than anything else, we must guard our hearts. Not coddle, pamper, or indulge—but *guard*. When I guard something, I protect it, watch over it, or take necessary precautions to keep it safe. We guard our hearts by running *away* from sin and running *to* God. Then we have a wellspring full of good things!

God Removes Stains

GOD'S TRUTH

For [the Lord] will be . . . like a strong soap that bleaches clothes. *Malachi 3:2*

No amount of soap or lye can make you clean.
Jeremiah 2:22

He gave his life to free us from every kind of sin, to cleanse us, and to make us his very own people, totally committed to doing good deeds. *Titus 2:14*

❀ I recently sat on something that stained my favorite pair of white capris. Although I sprayed them with stain remover and washed them with detergent, the spot didn't come out. Finally, I bleached the pants—and the stain was gone! Spots on my clothes are a nuisance, but stains in my heart present a much bigger problem. Only God can remove those. When we look to him for forgiveness, he promises to be—as Malachi says—like a strong soap that bleaches clothes!

PRAYER

Father, thank you for cleansing my heart. Amen.

Sometimes Loving Is Difficult

GOD'S ENCOURAGEMENT

Imitate God, therefore, in everything you do, because you are his dear children. Live a life filled with love, following the example of Christ. He loved us and offered himself as a sacrifice for us, a pleasing aroma to God. *Ephesians 5:1-2*

❀ Sometimes showing love to a family member is difficult. Jesus understands. When he gave himself as a sacrifice for sinners—for us—he wasn't treated well by mankind. He was crucified. But he loved us so much that he *died* for us! What does sacrificial love look like? It sometimes involves forfeiting a dream, a comfort, or a convenience, but loving our families the way God loved us brings great joy—to us and to God.

PRAYER

Father, help us to love like you love. Amen.

God Restores Our Hearts

GOD'S ASSURANCE

The LORD will guide you continually, giving you water when you are dry and restoring your strength. You will be like a well-watered garden, like an ever-flowing spring. Some of you will rebuild the deserted ruins of your cities. Then you will be known as a rebuilder of walls and a restorer of homes. *Isaiah 58:11-12*

❀ Last night my husband and I took a walk around the local lagoon. Because we've had so little rain this month, parts of the lagoon now expose mounds of dirt where there used to be water. I'm hoping rain will fall soon and the water level will be restored. *Restore,* meaning to reestablish or strengthen, is such a hopeful word. As we turn to God, he provides strength for our weakness, peace for our anxiety, and hope for our despair.

PRAYER

Father, please bring your restoration power to my heart. Amen.

A Secure Inheritance

GOD'S HOPE

And we have a priceless inheritance—an inheritance that is kept in heaven for you, pure and undefiled, beyond the reach of change and decay. And through your faith, God is protecting you by his power until you receive this salvation, which is ready to be revealed on the last day for all to see.

1 Peter 1:4-5

❀ While my husband was on business in Denver, Colorado, one son was traveling to the East Coast and another was in London, England (the day after the London subway bombings). Do I pray for each one to be protected while they travel? You bet! I never take their safe travel for granted. But I'm also thankful that through faith in Christ, each family member has the assurance of eternal life. There's tremendous comfort in knowing that God is holding each of us securely in his hands.

Cultivated Hearts

GOD'S TRUTH

"Plant the good seeds of righteousness, and you will harvest a crop of love. Plow up the hard ground of your hearts, for now is the time to seek the LORD, that he may come and shower righteousness upon you." But you have cultivated wickedness and harvested a thriving crop of sins.

Hosea 10:12-13

❀ While I'm outside walking, I enjoy admiring gardens that have been carefully cultivated. It's not as much fun to walk past gardens that have been neglected and have become a thriving patch of weeds. Hosea, an Old Testament prophet, used the picture of gardening to help us see that without God, our hearts will harvest crops of sin and destruction. When we ask God to cultivate our hearts, though, he will shower us with his righteousness, and our hearts will grow into a beautiful garden!

God Listens to Us

GOD'S ENCOURAGEMENT

Come and listen, all you who fear God, and I will tell you what he did for me. For I cried out to him for help, praising him as I spoke. If I had not confessed the sin in my heart, the Lord would not have listened. But God did listen! He paid attention to my prayer. *Psalm 66:16-19*

❁ When I have the opportunity to meet famous people, I'm not so amazed that they would speak to me, but I am impressed when they listen to me. Unlike some corporate executives who cloister themselves away from their employees, God opens his ears to his children. How comforting to know that the God who created the world and died for me also listens to me! Be encouraged today that God hears you.

PRAYER

Father, thank you for listening to me. I want to speak to you frequently. Amen.

God Sprinkles Our Hearts

GOD'S ASSURANCE

Then I will sprinkle clean water on you, and you will be clean. Your filth will be washed away, and you will no longer worship idols. And I will give you a new heart, and I will put a new spirit in you. *Ezekiel 36:25-26*

❀ When I was a child, my mom used to put out the sprinkler on hot summer days. What fun we kids had running, jumping, and sliding on the lawn. When we were done, we were usually covered with blades of grass. Then my mom sprinkled *us* to clean us up! The Old Testament prophet Ezekiel announced that God wants to sprinkle our hearts to clean us up, too. He wants to wash our sins away, give us a new heart for God, and place his Spirit within us. Through faith in Christ, God sprinkles our hearts and provides us with all these blessings!

God Promises to Sustain Us

GOD'S PROMISE

LORD, sustain me as you promised, that I may live! Do not let my hope be crushed. Sustain me, and I will be rescued; then I will meditate continually on your decrees. . . . Let me live so I can praise you, and may your regulations help me.

Psalm 119:116-117, 175

❀ Any mom who plays the piano knows that if you depress the pedal on the right, you will *sustain* whatever notes you choose to play. The sound will keep going. Without the pedal, it can be difficult to connect the notes. Moms might wish it were that simple to keep *ourselves* going! We can be thankful that sustaining power is within reach. When you feel tired, grab onto God. Grab onto his Word. When God sustains us, he does the work. He promises to keep us going as we look to him.

Wisdom Is Better than Jewelry

God's Wisdom

Joyful is the person who finds wisdom, the one who gains understanding. For wisdom is more profitable than silver, and her wages are better than gold. Wisdom is more precious than rubies; nothing you desire can compare with her.

Proverbs 3:13-15

✿ At a banquet years ago, I won a sapphire and diamond pendant that hangs on a delicate gold chain. As fond as I am of the necklace, God's Word tells me that wisdom is even more valuable than precious stones or gold. Nothing can compare with it. Although wisdom cannot be won at a banquet, Proverbs 1:7 tells us where to look: "How does a man become wise? The first step is to trust and reverence the Lord!" (TLB). God's Word has given us clear steps to follow as we seek to become wise. If we *really* want wisdom and if we look for it, we will find it.

Protect Your Luster

GOD'S GUIDANCE

Do everything without complaining and arguing, so that no one can criticize you. Live clean, innocent lives as children of God, shining like bright lights in a world full of crooked and perverse people. *Philippians 2:14-15*

A servant of the Lord must not quarrel but must be kind to everyone. *2 Timothy 2:24*

✵ Although we don't like to hear our children complain and argue, isn't it ironic that we sometimes complain ourselves? When we do, we're a bit like a silver pitcher that has become dull and tarnished. We lose some of our luster before a watching family and a watching world. May God help us stay away from complaining and arguing so that we will reflect Christ more effectively.

PRAYER

Father, please forgive us for whining and grumbling. Help us instead to be grateful and praise you so that we reflect Christ to our children! Amen.

God Calls the Stars by Name

"To whom will you compare me? Who is my equal?" asks the Holy One. Look up into the heavens. Who created all the stars? He brings them out like an army, one after another, calling each by its name. Because of his great power and incomparable strength, not a single one is missing.

Isaiah 40:25-26

❀ On a night when the sky is crystal clear, take your child outside, sit on a blanket together, and ask him or her to guess how many stars you can see. According to John Hawley of Argonne National Laboratory, an average galaxy contains ten billion stars. Because we can observe about ten billion galaxies in the universe, that's about one-hundred billion billion stars! Isaiah 40 tells us that God names each star. Won't it be incredible in heaven to hear God call each one by name? We serve an amazing God.

Behavior Speaks Louder Than Words

GOD'S GUIDANCE

Wives, in the same way be submissive to your husbands so that, if any of them do not believe the word, they may be won over without words by the behavior of their wives, when they see the purity and reverence of your lives.

1 Peter 3:1-2, NIV

❀ Some interpret these verses as handing a wife the role of a doormat, but when we take a closer look, that's not what we find. A wife is not a powerless woman; rather, she is much more powerful than she sometimes realizes. The woman who thinks she can persuade her husband only with *words* is missing something. Her husband is probably influenced more by the way she conducts herself—her ethics, her habits, her purity, and her interactions with others. If you're struggling with an issue with your husband, ask God to help you communicate lovingly through your actions.

The Treasure Is Christ!

GOD'S ENCOURAGEMENT

I want [believers] to be encouraged and knit together by strong ties of love. I want them to have complete confidence that they understand God's mysterious plan, which is Christ himself. In him lie hidden all the treasures of wisdom and knowledge. . . . I rejoice that . . . your faith in Christ is strong. *Colossians 2:2-3, 5*

❁ My husband and I will soon be empty nesters. In recent weeks, Jim and I have talked about things we are grateful we have done as parents, and things we wish we had done differently. You can imagine our appreciation, then, when we received these written thoughts from one son: "Thanks for bringing me up well, paying for my college education, and modeling your faith through the years. Even if the only thing you had passed on to me was Christ, I would still come out ahead—far ahead." We are grateful that he has Christ!

God Strengthens Us

GOD'S ASSURANCE

God arms me with strength, and he makes my way perfect. He makes me as surefooted as a deer, enabling me to stand on mountain heights. *Psalm 18:32-33*

The Sovereign LORD is my strength! He makes me as surefooted as a deer, able to tread upon the heights.

Habakkuk 3:19

When I was a child and my family vacationed in Door County, Wisconsin, we had fun counting deer. Tremendously agile, deer have been known to run at speeds of forty miles per hour. A deer who is running from a predator or trying to jump a fence can clear a span of twenty-five to thirty feet! It's no wonder that the Bible describes these animals as being sure-footed—strong, stable, and steady. I'm thankful that the Bible assures us that we can be *like* deer! As we look to God, he shares his strength with us, helping us to be stable and steady too.

God Wants to Draw Us Close

GOD'S COMFORT

Long ago the LORD said to Israel: "I have loved you, my people, with an everlasting love. With unfailing love I have drawn you to myself." *Jeremiah 31:3*

Remember, O LORD, your compassion and unfailing love, which you have shown from long ages past. *Psalm 25:6*

✿ When my sons were learning how to walk, I sometimes stood a distance away, stretched out my arms, and smiled with delight when they ran to me. I held out my arms because I wanted to draw them close. That is the picture Jeremiah paints of God (Jeremiah 31:3). Throughout history, God has reached toward each of us with his compassion and love. Although we don't physically see his arms or feel them wrap around us, he fills our hearts with his love. How? Through the presence of his Holy Spirit—one of his gifts to all who believe in Christ.

Time to Pray

GOD'S DIRECTION

Pray in the Spirit at all times and on every occasion. Stay alert and be persistent in your prayers for all believers everywhere. *Ephesians 6:18*

Be earnest and disciplined in your prayers. *1 Peter 4:7*

Always be joyful. Never stop praying.
1 Thessalonians 5:16-17

❀ Ken Taylor, the man who paraphrased *The Living Bible*, died recently. At his memorial service, Paul Mathews, a Tyndale House executive vice president, shared the following remembrance: "At the end of my meetings with Dr. Taylor each Wednesday afternoon, Ken would say, 'Don't leave yet! If we have time to talk about these issues and time to worry about these issues, then we have time to *pray* about them.' And we always did." What a great idea for moms, too. If you've been talking or worrying about certain issues, pray about them today. God hears us!

A Close Relationship with God

GOD'S HOPE

I am the way, the truth, and the life. No one can come to the Father except through me. *John 14:6*

God showed how much he loved us by sending his one and only Son into the world so that we might have eternal life through him. *1 John 4:9*

❀ Pose the following situation to your child: Imagine that you're hiking, and you come upon a wide river. A forest ranger informs you there's only one bridge to get you where you need to go. Instead of complaining that there's only one bridge, you'd probably be grateful that there *is* a bridge! For that same reason, I'm thankful that Jesus has bridged the gap to God.

PRAYER

Father, thank you that we can enjoy a relationship with you because Jesus died for our sins. Amen.

Christ's Power in Our Weakness

GOD'S PROMISE

Each time [the Lord] said, "My grace is all you need. My power works best in weakness." So now I am glad to boast about my weaknesses, so that the power of Christ can work through me. *2 Corinthians 12:9*

For I can do everything through Christ, who gives me strength. *Philippians 4:13*

❀ When I encounter problems in my life, too often my initial approach is to work hard at being strong. But I have discovered that even the best of my strength is no match for many of my challenges as a mom. The apostle Paul is a great example of a person God was able to use to further his Kingdom. But 2 Corinthians 12:9 makes it clear that it wasn't because Paul was strong. God can use us when we admit our weakness before him, asking him to strengthen us for the increase of *his* Kingdom, not ours.

Does God *Really* Know
What He's Doing?

GOD'S TRUTH

The LORD's plans stand firm forever; his intentions can never be shaken. *Psalm 33:11*

The power of your right hand saves me. The LORD will work out his plans for my life—for your faithful love, O LORD, endures forever. Don't abandon me, for you made me.

Psalm 138:7-8

❀ Perhaps your husband is looking for a job, or some medical tests on your child suggest a serious problem, or your parent in another state needs help. At times when we feel we've been blindsided, it's comforting to be reminded that God is in control and that he has good purposes for us and for our children. *Nothing* can threaten his purposes for us!

PRAYER

Father, thank you that even when things in my life feel out of control, you are always in charge. Amen.

In the Midst of Life, Make Disciples

GOD'S CHALLENGE

Therefore, go and make disciples of all the nations, baptizing them in the name of the Father and the Son and the Holy Spirit. Teach these new disciples to obey all the commands I have given you. And be sure of this: I am with you always, even to the end of the age. *Matthew 28:19-20*

❀ We often equate this passage with missionaries who serve in a foreign country. But these verses hold special meaning for us as moms. While we are "doing life," Jesus wants us to make disciples—of our children, first, and also of others around us. We can do some of this during the day in, day out experiences of life. Other disciplines—Bible reading, Bible memorization, and prayer—can be planned into our schedules on a more regular basis. However we do it, God equips us for the task and promises us his presence!

Don't Anger Your Children

Do not provoke your children to anger by the way you treat them. Rather, bring them up with the discipline and instruction that comes from the Lord. *Ephesians 6:4*

Do not aggravate your children, or they will become discouraged. *Colossians 3:21*

❀ Have you ever had "girdling" problems with a plant? Maybe it was tied down too tightly with a wire or rope and became choked. Girdling can happen when stemmed plants have been restrained so much that there is not enough room for them to grow. Girdling can happen with children, too. I know there were times when my expectations were so high or my attitude so impatient that my children were provoked to anger or discouragement. When this happens we can offer an apology or a humble request for forgiveness, along with an assurance that we don't want to provoke them like that again.

When Suffering Comes, Ask "Who?" Instead of "Why?"

GOD'S ENCOURAGEMENT

We give great honor to those who endure under suffering.
James 5:11

We can rejoice, too, when we run into problems and trials, for we know that they help us develop endurance. And endurance develops strength of character, and character strengthens our confident hope of salvation. *Romans 5:3-4*

❀ Do you have a child who is going through emotional or physical turmoil? Are you experiencing financial difficulties? Do you ever feel like throwing in the towel? Suffering—especially when it is ongoing—can wear us down and challenge our perspectives. But it can also produce unique opportunities for service to Christ that wouldn't be possible if we hadn't suffered and persevered—imperfect as our perseverance might be. When suffering comes, we won't always know the answer to the question, *Why?* but we do know whom to run to for strength to persevere.

PRAYER

God, please help us to trust you, keep going, and never give up. Amen.

We Are in Good Hands

GOD'S TRUTH

Who kept the sea inside its boundaries as it burst from the womb, and as I clothed it with clouds and wrapped it in thick darkness? . . . Have you explored the springs from which the seas come? Have you explored their depths? . . . Do you realize the extent of the earth? *Job 38:8-9, 16, 18*

❀ Just east of the island of Guam, the *Marianas Trench* is the deepest known depression on the earth's surface. If you dropped a heavy anchor into the Pacific Ocean directly over the Marianas Trench, one hour later the anchor might not have touched bottom because the floor of the depression is located seven miles beneath the water's surface! I am grateful that the God who "holds in his hands the depths of the earth" (Psalm 95:4) also holds my children and me in his hands (see Psalm 66:9).

Know God through Christ

GOD'S ASSURANCE

Therefore, since we have been made right in God's sight by faith, we have peace with God because of what Jesus Christ our Lord has done for us. Because of our faith, Christ has brought us into this place of undeserved privilege where we now stand, and we confidently and joyfully look forward to sharing God's glory. *Romans 5:1-2*

❀ We might think that a lot of people in the world know God—if the determining factor were how much they mention his name. I sometimes wonder if people who frequently say, "For God's sake!" have any idea that they can actually know God through Jesus Christ. The whole story of the Bible shows how God took initiative to bring us to himself through Christ. Christ has paved the way for us to know God!

PRAYER

Lord, thank you for allowing us to know you. Amen.

God's Way of Seeing

GOD'S DIRECTION

Peter took [Jesus] aside and began to reprimand him for saying such things. Jesus turned around and looked at his disciples, then reprimanded Peter. . . . "You are seeing things merely from a human point of view, not from God's." *Mark 8:32-33*

❀ Having a positive outlook isn't too difficult on a hot day when the air conditioner's working, all my relationships are humming along smoothly, and my children are behaving themselves. But when things go sour, perspective sometimes dims. When Jesus announced to the disciples that he would be rejected and killed, and he would rise again, Peter scolded Jesus. I can't imagine telling Jesus he was wrong. But in reality, I do that, too, if I expect a happy life with no suffering. The world's goal is glory without suffering, but God's goal is to change suffering into glory. Whichever philosophy we accept will determine our perspective.

God's Handiwork Is Stunning

GOD'S HOPE

No eye has seen, no ear has heard, and no mind has imagined what God has prepared for those who love him.

1 Corinthians 2:9

For this world is not our permanent home; we are looking forward to a home yet to come. *Hebrews 13:14*

✿ Last summer, I spent a weekend in Cedar Rapids, Iowa, with my two sisters. While on a walk, we stumbled upon Noel Ridge, a sprawling park that contained acres of gorgeous flowers and ground covers—a gardener's delight. As I wandered around the colorful gardens, I found myself hoping that when I get to heaven I'll be able to admire every single flower and plant that God created. I can't imagine what it will be like to stroll through *that* garden. Which parts of God's handiwork would you and your children most like to admire in heaven?

Mothers of the Towel

GOD'S TRUTH

Jesus knew that the Father had given him authority over everything and that he had come from God and would return to God. So he got up from the table, took off his robe, wrapped a towel around his waist, and poured water into a basin. Then he began to wash the disciples' feet.

John 13:3-5

❀ Knowing the authority that God had given to Jesus, we might have expected Jesus to ask the disciples to wash *his* feet. But Jesus got up and washed the *disciples'* feet. Amazing! What's more, Jesus knew that Judas and Peter were about to betray and deny him, and he still washed their feet. Jesus demonstrated that his posture (service) flowed out of his position (he came from God and would return to God). Moms can demonstrate that service too. It was Jesus' steadfast relationship with the Father that prompted him to serve. A secure relationship with the heavenly Father motivates moms to serve too.

Depending on Our Creator

GOD'S GUIDANCE

What sorrow awaits those who argue with their Creator. Does a clay pot argue with its maker? Does the clay dispute with the one who shapes it, saying, "Stop, you're doing it wrong!" Does the pot exclaim, "How clumsy can you be?"

Isaiah 45:9

❀ I enjoy displaying several clay pots my sons crafted for me at various stages of their childhood. Perhaps you have a few in your home, too. It's humorous to imagine one of those pots shouting back to our children, "Stop, you're doing it wrong!" or "How clumsy can you be?" We know that would never happen. But sometimes we're tempted to think that way about God's dealing in our lives—especially when we're confused and don't have a clue what he's doing. Oh, that we would remember that God is our Creator, and that our very existence depends on him!

Remember God's Benefits

GOD'S ENCOURAGEMENT
Praise the LORD, O my soul, and forget not all his benefits.
Psalm 103:2, NIV

God has united you with Christ Jesus. For our benefit God made him to be wisdom itself. Christ made us right with God; he made us pure and holy, and he freed us from sin.
1 Corinthians 1:30

❀ The fifth-grade girls in my church recently memorized Psalm 103 and recited it together in a Sunday service. The girls will probably remember the words about God's *benefits* for the rest of their lives. That's encouraging to see, especially when children in our society sometimes grow up with a sense of entitlement instead of gratitude. A benefit is an advantage, an asset, or a blessing—something that makes our lives better. One time this week when you pray with your children, discuss some of God's benefits together.

Models of Hard Work

GOD'S DIRECTION

Take a lesson from the ants, you lazybones. Learn from their ways and become wise! Though they have no prince or governor or ruler to make them work, they labor hard all summer, gathering food for the winter. *Proverbs 6:6-8*

The LORD gives his people strength. *Psalm 29:11*

❀ Although ants are small, they are very wise. They almost make us look lazy. They work night and day, they store up food, and they build their mounds three or four times higher (comparatively speaking) than the Egyptian pyramids are to us. When ants are sick, they care for each other, and in the winter they eat the food they saved in the summer. We can learn a lot about diligence and foresight from the ants.

PRAYER

Father, give us the energy and the desire to work hard for you and our families. Amen.

Look Ahead

GOD'S HOPE

This is my second letter to you, dear friends, and in both of them I have tried to stimulate your wholesome thinking and refresh your memory. . . . But we are looking forward to the new heavens and new earth he has promised, a world filled with God's righteousness. *2 Peter 3:1, 13*

❀ I treasure my old photo albums. But they sometimes bring back memories of losses or painful circumstances surrounding the times when the pictures were taken. How do we put those situations into perspective? By refreshing our memories about why we're here and looking forward to what's ahead. We are here on earth to do the work that God has called us to do, and we look forward to a time when no sorrows or pain will exist. Because of the Good News of Christ, we can look forward to heaven.

Remember!

GOD'S TRUTH

I remember your wonderful deeds of long ago. They are constantly in my thoughts. I cannot stop thinking about your mighty works. *Psalm 77:11-12*

I remember the days of old. I ponder all your great works and think about what you have done. *Psalm 143:5*

❀ I remember a time of pain and sadness that I neither wanted nor understood. I decided to get alone for one day of thinking, praying, and pacing the floor with open Bible in hand. As I read accounts of people in the Bible who encountered seemingly impossible circumstances, I sensed God's presence and strength washing over me. The common denominator in those accounts was that the characters *remembered* things God had done in the past. As we ponder what he has done and cry out to him for help in our present situations, we, too, are stirred to trust him.

Praising God Lifts Our Hearts

GOD'S ENCOURAGEMENT

The LORD is my strength and shield. I trust him with all my heart. He helps me, and my heart is filled with joy. I burst out in songs of thanksgiving. *Psalm 28:7*

Shout to the LORD, all the earth; break out in praise and sing for joy! *Psalm 98:4*

❀ As a child, I was frequently blessed to hear hymns and praise songs sung by George Beverly Shea—my mother's favorite vocalist. One of Shea's favorites was a song that *his* mother awakened him with each morning as a child: "Singing I go along life's road, praising the Lord, praising the Lord; Singing I go along life's road, for Jesus has lifted my load." I can't think of any better words for a child to wake up to in the morning! As you share your favorite songs with your children, look for lyrics that will encourage them and provide examples of praise.

Hope = Waiting on God

GOD'S HOPE

We wait in hope for the LORD; he is our help and our shield.
In him our hearts rejoice, for we trust in his holy name.
May your unfailing love rest upon us, O LORD, even as we
put our hope in you. *Psalm 33:20-22, NIV*

❀ Waiting is difficult. The Old Testament character
Joseph spent a fair amount of his life waiting—first in the
dry well where his brothers dumped him before they sold
him to Ishmaelite traders, and then after he was imprisoned
by Potiphar, one of Pharaoh's officials. But the Bible tells us
that God was with Joseph and that Joseph experienced success in all that he did. While we wait, it's helpful to remember that we're not just waiting on people or a process—
we're waiting on God.

PRAYER

Father, thanks for the encouragement of other people who
waited on you and saw you act—in your own perfect time.
Amen.

Light Illumines

GOD'S TRUTH

No one lights a lamp and then covers it with a bowl or hides it under a bed. A lamp is placed on a stand, where its light can be seen by all who enter the house. *Luke 8:16*

A lamp is placed on a stand, where its light will shine.
Mark 4:21

❀ When I was a child, evening thunderstorms were not something to fear—they were cause for great excitement. Why? It was a chance to light candles! My mom would scurry around the house collecting candles and matches, bringing them to the dining room table. Then, we would light them and deliver them to various rooms in the house, just in case the lights went out—and of course we hoped they would. In the same way that candles give off light for everyone in the house, our lives give off the light of Christ when his truth illumines our lives.

God Is Our Protective Shade

GOD'S ENCOURAGEMENT

The LORD himself watches over you! The LORD stands beside you as your protective shade. The sun will not harm you by day, nor the moon at night. . . . The LORD keeps watch over you as you come and go, both now and forever.

Psalm 121:5-6, 8

As I write this devotional, the Chicago area is experiencing a heat wave. When I have taken my morning walks or watered flowers these past few days, I've looked for shady spots to provide some protection from the heat of the sun. In Psalm 121, God declares himself to be our protective shade. I can relate to that image! These verses encourage me that not only is God watching over me, but that he's also doing it *all the time*—day and night, when I'm coming and going, both now and forever. He watches over *me!*

Hope Comes with Remembering

God's Hope

For he issued his laws to Jacob; he gave his instructions to Israel. He commanded our ancestors to teach them to their children, so the next generation might know them—even the children not yet born—and they in turn will teach their own children. So each generation should set its hope anew on God, not forgetting his glorious miracles and obeying his commands. *Psalm 78:5-7*

✿ When we remember how God provided for his people in the past, we can be strengthened to face difficulties. If God could make the waters of the Red Sea stand up like walls (Psalm 78:13), split open rocks in the wilderness to gush with water (v. 15), and rain down bread from the heavens (v. 24), then certainly he can take care of us.

Prayer

Father, I'm glad that we can read stories of your power and provision over and over again in the Bible. Thank you for these encouraging reminders. Amen.

In the Midst of Fears, Look to God

GOD'S TRUTH

They spread this bad report about the land among the Israelites: "The land we traveled through and explored will devour anyone who goes to live there. All the people we saw were huge. We even saw giants there, the descendants of Anak. Next to them we felt like grasshoppers, and that's what they thought, too!" *Numbers 13:32-33*

❈ Moses sent twelve spies into Canaan. Two of them said, "Let's go!" Ten said, "No, don't go—we felt like grasshoppers in comparison to the people who live in the land!" Sometimes moms feel as small as grasshoppers in the face of mounting challenges too. It can be tempting to mull over our fears instead of looking to God. Rehearsing God's promises, like Caleb and Joshua did, would be a better choice: "The Lord loves us, he keeps his promises, he is with us. Don't be afraid!"

God Is Our Strength

GOD'S PROMISE

David replied to the Philistine, "You come to me with sword, spear, and javelin, but I come to you in the name of the LORD of Heaven's Armies—the God of the armies of Israel, whom you have defied. . . . And everyone assembled here will know that the LORD rescues his people, but not with sword and spear. This is the LORD's battle, and he will give you to us!" *1 Samuel 17:45-47*

David depended on God's strength when he confronted the seemingly impossible power of the giant Goliath. Sometimes moms encounter situations that feel impossible too. Like David, we can pray persistently for the honor of God's name and wait to see evidence of his strength in a battle that is not ours, but God's!

PRAYER

Lord Almighty, please show us evidence of your power and glory as we pray for the honor of your name. Amen.

Stirring Up Anger

God's Wisdom

As the beating of cream yields butter and striking the nose causes bleeding, so stirring up anger causes quarrels.

Proverbs 30:33

An angry person starts fights; a hot-tempered person commits all kinds of sin. *Proverbs 29:22*

Whipping cream and a clear jar are all you need to do an experiment (or "*con*speriment," as five-year-old Jordan used to say) with your children. If you shake one-half cup of real whipping cream in a clear glass jar with a tight-fitting lid, the cream will double in volume and eventually form butter. This can help demonstrate the danger of stirring up anger. The Bible tells us that just as certainly as beating cream results in butter, angry comments will escalate into quarrels.

Prayer

Father, when I'm tempted to speak angry words, help me to be self-disciplined and avoid starting a quarrel. Amen.

Be an Example

GOD'S CHALLENGE
You yourself must be an example to them by doing good works of every kind. Let everything you do reflect the integrity and seriousness of your teaching. *Titus 2:7*

And you should imitate me, just as I imitate Christ.
1 Corinthians 11:1

❀ One day I heard three-year-old Chad start to cry outside. I ran to the back door and saw that the piece of bread he had set down in his wagon was now being carried off in the beak of a big black crow! As I walked over to console Chad, he put his hands on his little waist and yelled up to the crow, "Birdie, what do you say?" Whether Chad wanted to hear "thank you" or "I'm sorry," clearly this crow needed to say something! It's rewarding to see young children follow the behavior we've modeled for them. We are examples to our children!

Doing God's Repair Work

Hezekiah was twenty-five years old when he became the king of Judah. . . . He did what was pleasing in the LORD's sight. . . . In the very first month of the first year of his reign, Hezekiah reopened the doors of the Temple of the LORD and repaired them. *2 Chronicles 29:1-3*

❀ King Hezekiah's father had shut the doors of the Temple so no one could worship there. So when Hezekiah became king, one of his first actions was to make necessary repairs. There are times in our lives when God graciously points out the need for heart repairs. Perhaps there are actions we would be wise to do more—or less—of. Giving attention to necessary heart repairs not only pleases God but also improves quality of life—both for us and for our families.

We Need Others

GOD'S GUIDANCE

Elisha said, "Borrow as many empty jars as you can from your friends and neighbors." *2 Kings 4:3*

A friend is always loyal, and a brother is born to help in time of need. *Proverbs 17:17*

❀ The widow mentioned in 2 Kings 4 was instructed by Elisha to ask all her friends and neighbors for jars. Why? They would hold the oil that was about to be miraculously multiplied. Asking for help may have felt risky and humbling to the widow, but imagine the joy everyone shared in the experience.

God built into us the need for friendship, intending for us to reach out to others. When we feel lonely, it's good to present our need to God, because he sees us and provides for us. But it's also good to call a friend and put a date on the calendar!

When Lonely, Run to God

GOD'S ENCOURAGEMENT

LORD, hear my prayer! Listen to my plea! Don't turn away from me in my time of distress. . . . I am like an owl in the desert, like a little owl in a far-off wilderness. I lie awake, lonely as a solitary bird on the roof. *Psalm 102:1-2, 6-7*

One morning the women's Bible study at my church had to be moved out of the sanctuary to another location. The reason? A single baby owl was flying around in the organ pipes! Owls are solitary birds, and even juvenile owls sometimes travel up to 150 miles alone. So when the psalmist said, "I am . . . like a little owl in a far-off wilderness," he was describing his loneliness—a feeling moms can relate to even when there are lots of little bodies around. When we feel lonely, we can run to God and be thankful he will never turn away.

Praise Changes Our Perspectives

GOD'S ASSURANCE

I will exalt you, my God and King, and praise your name forever and ever. . . . The LORD is close to all who call on him, yes, to all who call on him in truth. He grants the desires of those who fear him; he hears their cries for help and rescues them. *Psalm 145:1, 18-19*

❀ One of my friend's sons had a kindergarten teacher who was rather buxom. Since that word was not yet in the child's vocabulary, he described her to his parents by saying, "My teacher has two very heavy hearts!" His parents got the picture. When we *really* have a heavy, sorrowful heart, what should we do? The Psalms point to praising God because praise takes our minds off our problems and puts them on God. When we consider him, our perspectives change and we're better prepared to receive his love and help. Praise is powerful!

God's Presence Brings Peace

GOD'S COMFORT

In peace I will lie down and sleep, for you alone, O LORD, will keep me safe. *Psalm 4:8*

He will not let you stumble; the one who watches over you will not slumber. . . . The LORD keeps watch over you as you come and go, both now and forever. *Psalm 121:3, 8*

We read in Mark 4 that Jesus and his disciples were in a boat on the Sea of Galilee when a fierce storm suddenly came up. In the middle of the storm, Jesus was able to continue napping. Why? Because he knew that God would care for him. Are you experiencing storms in your life? Are any of your children struggling at school or with friends? Remember that God wants us to come to him for refuge. *He* is our security. *He* is our peace.

PRAYER

Father, when we feel fearful, worried, or insecure, may we run to you, knowing that you want to give us your peace. Amen.

Talk about Success,
Talk about Mistakes

GOD'S DIRECTION

Listen, all who live in the land. In all your history, has anything like this happened before? Tell your children about it in the years to come, and let your children tell their children. Pass the story down from generation to generation.

Joel 1:2-3

The "story" referred to in Joel 1, which God wanted his people to pass on to the next generation, was not a happy piece of news. It spoke of God's judgment, not God's blessing. That's hard for most moms. We'd rather tell our children about a favorite family vacation than speak of a difficult memory or a painful family secret. But if sharing our painful experiences will help the next generation not to repeat them, they might be a worthy gift. If we're honest about the good *and* the bad, we present our children with an opportunity to repeat our successes but avoid our mistakes.

Jesus Saves

GOD'S HOPE

Return, O LORD, and rescue me. Save me because of your unfailing love. *Psalm 6:4*

Protect me, for I am devoted to you. Save me, for I serve you and trust you. You are my God. Be merciful to me, O Lord. *Psalm 86:2-3*

❀ I've heard nursing called a mother's "secret weapon." Those of you who have nursed your children understand. My baby could have been screaming at full volume, but if I picked him up and began nursing him, he stopped crying. I saved my baby from his distress. As wonderful as it feels for us to save our babies from hunger and tears, God sent Jesus to save us from much more than that. *Jesus* means "the Lord saves," and only he can save us from sin. Jesus came to be our Savior by dying on the cross for us. That's how much God loves *us!*

An Unfair Trade

For God made Christ, who never sinned, to be the offering
for our sin, so that we could be made right with God
through Christ. *2 Corinthians 5:21*

[God] himself is fair and just, and he declares sinners to be
right in his sight when they believe in Jesus. *Romans 3:26*

⊛ The online company eBay is built on the principle of
exchange: Put an item up for sale and wait to see what
another person is willing to pay for it. All of us make
exchanges every day—a couple dollars for a bagel or a cup of
coffee, several dollars for a gallon of milk, and so on. That's
not the case with righteousness. We can never earn enough
money to buy righteousness, nor can we ever do enough
good deeds to earn it. But gaining righteousness *does* involve
a trade of sorts. God trades his righteousness for *our* sin—
because he loves us. What a generous God!

A Cup of Cold Water

GOD'S CHALLENGE

If anyone gives you even a cup of water because you belong to the Messiah, I tell you the truth, that person will surely be rewarded. *Mark 9:41*

Remember that the Lord will reward each one of us for the good we do. *Ephesians 6:8*

For three years my oldest son, Chad, lived in an apartment in Chicago. Each day, he rode the subway to his job downtown, where he worked as a mechanical engineer. Because Chad passed needy people as he came and went, he decided that when he made a lunch for himself each morning, he'd also make an extra one to give away. Over the years, that added up to about eight hundred lunches. God loves it when we show love to others. With your children, consider sharing "a cup of cold water" with someone around you who needs encouragement or help.

Pray with Scripture

GOD'S TRUTH

So we have not stopped praying for you since we first heard about you. We ask God to give you complete knowledge of his will and to give you spiritual wisdom and understanding.

Colossians 1:9

I pray that your love will overflow more and more, and that you will keep on growing in knowledge and understanding.

Philippians 1:9

❀ Mary, one of my friends from church, hosted a prayer time one fall for moms whose children had gone off to college. We enjoyed a wonderful time of interceding together for the needs of our children. What made it particularly special was that Mary suggested we use Scripture (like the verses above) to pray back to God some of the specific ways he wants us all to grow to be more like him. Whether we're praying for our children, our husbands, or ourselves, I'm thankful that God's words add power to our prayers.

Joy Follows Obedience

GOD'S GUIDANCE

When you obey my commandments, you remain in my love, just as I obey my Father's commandments and remain in his love. I have told you these things so that you will be filled with my joy. Yes, your joy will overflow!

John 15:10-11

Light shines on the godly, and joy on those whose hearts are right. *Psalm 97:11*

Evil people are trapped by sin, but the righteous escape, shouting for joy. *Proverbs 29:6*

Has your son ever escaped getting hit by a car because he obeyed your instructions not to cross the street? Has your daughter escaped getting an electric shock because she listened when you said, "Don't touch the outlet"? That kind of obedience brings joy. We, too, can shout for joy when we flee the traps of sin and choose to obey God.

PRAYER

Father, I long to experience your overflowing joy. Please strengthen me to obey you. Amen.

Look for God's Mercies

GOD'S ENCOURAGEMENT

The faithful love of the LORD never ends! His mercies never cease. Great is his faithfulness; his mercies begin afresh each morning. *Lamentations 3:22-23*

Each day the LORD pours his unfailing love upon me, and through each night I sing his songs, praying to God who gives me life. *Psalm 42:8*

❀ Imagine that you have given your children a bowl of sand and asked them to find the particles of iron in it. They might look with their eyes or dig with their fingers, but they wouldn't be able to detect the iron. If, however, they swept a magnet through the sand, the iron particles would be irresistibly drawn to it. An unthankful heart is like fingers trying to sift through the sand—it doesn't discover God's mercies. But a thankful heart, just like the magnet, sweeps through life's circumstances and finds daily blessings from God.

We Can Be Consistently Joyful

GOD'S ASSURANCE

Many people say, "Who will show us better times?" Let your face smile on us, LORD. You have given me greater joy than those who have abundant harvests of grain and new wine. *Psalm 4:6-7*

I know the LORD is always with me. I will not be shaken, for he is right beside me. No wonder my heart is glad, and I rejoice. My body rests in safety. *Psalm 16:8-9*

✿ Happiness comes easily on the heels of good news about a child's award or a long-anticipated vacation, but bad news doesn't prompt the same feelings. Joy, unlike happiness, is available to believers in Christ even in the middle of difficult circumstances. It's a fruit of the Holy Spirit's presence in our lives. Even in the midst of difficulties, moms can experience joy by drawing close to Christ.

Christ, Our Secure Anchor

GOD'S HOPE

So God has given both his promise and his oath. These two things are unchangeable because it is impossible for God to lie. Therefore, we who have fled to him for refuge can have great confidence as we hold to the hope that lies before us. This hope is a strong and trustworthy anchor for our souls.

Hebrews 6:18-19

When my family snorkeled in the Virgin Islands, our boat captain located his favorite spot and dropped an anchor. An anchor—which holds the boat securely in place—is used in the Bible to give a strong picture of our hope in Christ. Because Christ died, rose again, and now lives in heaven, our lives can be anchored, not to the bottom of the ocean, but to the very throne of God! Our hope of refuge and safety for now and for eternity is secure and immovable because it is anchored in *Christ*.

Holding Firm to God's Word

GOD'S CHALLENGE

You can be sure that no immoral, impure, or greedy person will inherit the Kingdom of Christ and of God. For a greedy person is an idolater, worshiping the things of this world. Don't be fooled by those who try to excuse these sins.

Ephesians 5:5-6

Chameleons are a specialized group of lizards. Perhaps the most interesting thing about them is their ability to change the color of their skin—usually for camouflage purposes. Camouflage makes it possible for a chameleon to stalk its prey and hide from its predators. For the Christian, though, camouflage is a problem. Ephesians 5 cautions us about human chameleons and warns us not to be fooled by those who try to excuse sexual immorality, impurity, or greed. When we're tempted to ignore our convictions, we can ask God for the courage and faith to hold firm.

Our Creator Helps Us Know How to Live

GOD'S TRUTH

Do you know the laws of the universe? Can you use them to regulate the earth? Can you shout to the clouds and make it rain? Can you make lightning appear and cause it to strike as you direct? Who gives intuition to the heart and instinct to the mind? *Job 38:33-36*

❀ Question: Who planned that the proboscis monkey would live only on the island of Borneo in Southeast Asia? Answer: the God who also prompts those monkeys to make loud honking sounds when they sense danger. Question: Who taught proboscis monkeys that 95 percent of their diet would come from mangrove and pedada leaves? Answer: God, who created them to swim without splashing. Question: Whom can we trust to help us know how to live? Answer: the same creative God who created the proboscis monkey and taught it how to live!

New Attitudes

GOD'S GUIDANCE

Now your attitudes and thoughts must all be constantly changing for the better. Yes, you must be a new and different person, holy and good. Clothe yourself with this new nature. *Ephesians 4:23-24,* TLB

May God . . . help you live in complete harmony with each other, as is fitting for followers of Christ Jesus. *Romans 15:5*

✿ Throughout the Bible are references to taking off one garment and putting on a new, clean one. God has given us a new wardrobe, but it's possible for a believer—a new person in Christ—to revert to wearing the dirty clothing of the old person. On days when I am impatient or I yell at my children, new garments sound wonderful! I'm thankful that, as we spend time in God's Word and ask him for his help, we can see growth in our attitudes and thoughts.

All of My Heart

GOD'S ENCOURAGEMENT

And now, Israel, what does the LORD your God require of you? He requires only that you fear the LORD your God, and live in a way that pleases him, and love him and serve him with all your heart and soul. *Deuteronomy 10:12*

I love God's law with all my heart. *Romans 7:22*

"Next, we'll stir in *all* of the flour." "Please pick up *all* of your toys." "Did you take out *all* of the trash?" Sound familiar? We're not satisfied with halfhearted attempts. If I were to give one of my children forty-nine pennies to throw into a toll machine that requires fifty cents, the gate wouldn't go up—until *all* fifty cents were thrown in. God asks for all of us, too—not because he's an exacting taskmaster, but because he has our best interests at heart. He will help us love him with our whole hearts.

Integrity Protects

GOD'S ASSURANCE

The godly walk with integrity; blessed are their children who follow them. *Proverbs 20:7*

May integrity and honesty protect me, for I put my hope in you. *Psalm 25:21*

I know, my God, that you examine our hearts and rejoice when you find integrity there. *1 Chronicles 29:17*

❀ Recently I walked by a church whose parking lot signs gave conflicting messages. As I entered the driveway, a street sign read ONE WAY ONLY. But the pavement under my feet showed two distinct lanes, one with an arrow pointing toward me and one with an arrow pointing away. I left the parking lot wondering how many times my life has sent mixed messages to my children. Maybe I encourage my children to be patient with a friend, but I get impatient with them. I don't want my children to be perplexed by conflicting signs in my life. Integrity pleases God and protects us!

Wait Expectantly

GOD'S HOPE

O LORD, hear me as I pray; pay attention to my groaning. Listen to my cry for help, my King and my God, for I pray to no one but you. Listen to my voice in the morning, LORD. Each morning I bring my requests to you and wait expectantly. *Psalm 5:1-3*

All moms are waiting and hoping for something—whether it's a new stage in our children's development or a positive change in a relationship. What can we do while we're waiting? In Psalm 5:1-3, the psalmist suggests three things we can ask *God* to do and five things that *we* can do. We ask God to (1) hear, (2) pay attention, and (3) listen to us. Some things we can do are (1) pray, (2) groan, (3) cry, (4) bring our requests to God, and (5) wait expectantly. In the same way that a pregnant mother anticipates the birth of her child, we can wait, hope, and anticipate God's help in our lives.

Redeeming Mercy

GOD'S TRUTH

Once we, too, were foolish and disobedient. We were mis-led and became slaves to many lusts and pleasures. . . . But—"When God our Savior revealed his kindness and love, he saved us, not because of the righteous things we had done, but because of his mercy." *Titus 3:3-5*

❁ When I was a child, my parents collected S & H Green Stamps, which were given in return for purchases made at various stores. When a whole book was filled with stamps, it could be redeemed for a gift of the customer's choice. God's redemption is surprisingly different. Jesus Christ chose to die for us not because of anything good we had done but because of his mercy. When we believe, he gives us the washing of rebirth and the renewal of the Holy Spirit, treats us as though we had never sinned, and calls us God's children. God's redeeming mercy is an indescribable gift!

Following Directions
Can Save Lives

GOD'S GUIDANCE

Even after all the young women had been transferred to the second harem and Mordecai had become a palace official, Esther continued to keep her family background and nationality a secret. She was still following Mordecai's directions, just as she did when she lived in his home.

Esther 2:19-20

※ Esther followed Mordecai's directions, "just as she did when she lived in his home." Those words are music to a mom's ears! We all want our children to follow our directions. Whether it's moms telling kids not to play with matches or Mordecai instructing Esther to keep quiet about her national identity until the right time, following instructions can save lives. Based on what we know about Mordecai from the Old Testament book of Esther, it seems he treated his cousin Esther with thoughtfulness, love, and respect—a good example for moms who want their children to follow directions too!

God Is Faithful

For the LORD is good. His unfailing love continues forever,
and his faithfulness continues to each generation.

Psalm 100:5

Give thanks to the LORD and proclaim his greatness. Let the
whole world know what he has done. . . . Tell everyone
about his wonderful deeds. *Psalm 105:1-2*

✸ Do you have certain people or things in your life that
remind you of how much you have to be thankful for?
When I see my youngest son running around, I realize how
thankful I am that his left femur mended after a skateboard-
ing accident. Whenever I see or hear from our young friend
Drew, I'm thankful that God healed his body after a three-
year bout with leukemia.

When we take time to recall God's faithfulness, we will
be encouraged and renewed.

PRAYER

God, thank you for seeing and providing. Thanks for specific
events in our lives that strengthen our faith in you. Amen.

Passport of Faith

GOD'S TRUTH

For this world is not our permanent home; we are looking forward to a home yet to come. *Hebrews 13:14*

Abraham was confidently looking forward to a city with eternal foundations, a city designed and built by God.
Hebrews 11:10

❀ Because my husband and one of my sons travel internationally, they use their passports frequently. I enjoy paging through their passports and seeing stamps from England, Indonesia, Germany, the Philippines, Hungary, India, Australia, Israel, New Zealand, Thailand, and other locations. Believers in Christ are headed to the eternal city of heaven when we depart our temporary locations on the earth. Our passports won't help us enter that city, though. What we need is faith in Jesus' death and resurrection—faith that causes us to die to sin and live to righteousness. Faith is our passport to the city of heaven!

From Rags to Righteousness

GOD'S ENCOURAGEMENT

We are all infected and impure with sin. When we display our righteous deeds, they are nothing but filthy rags.

Isaiah 64:6

We have been rescued from our enemies so we can serve God without fear, in holiness and righteousness for as long as we live. *Luke 1:74-75*

✿ When I was a child, Cinderella was one of my favorite fairy tale characters. If her fairy godmother hadn't stepped in to help, Cinderella wouldn't have had a lovely gown to wear to the ball. Up until that point, all she owned were raggedy clothes. We're a bit like Cinderella in that sense. Whether we're kids or adults, God tells us that our best efforts are like rags to him. But the most wonderful news in the universe is that Christ has provided us with snow white garments of *his* righteousness. Let that thought encourage you today. God loves you enough to cleanse you completely!

Fight the Good Fight

GOD'S CHALLENGE

Pursue righteousness and a godly life, along with faith, love, perseverance, and gentleness. Fight the good fight for the true faith. Hold tightly to the eternal life to which God has called you, which you have confessed so well before many witnesses. *1 Timothy 6:11-12*

❀ When my three boys were young, it wasn't uncommon for me to say, "Please stop fighting!" or "Guys, cut it out!" Isn't it ironic, then, that in this devotional, I'm encouraging moms to fight? Not only do we struggle *against* our adversary, the devil, but we also strive vigorously *for* faith. As we fight against the pressures of the world, the flesh, and the devil through the power of God's Word and Spirit, we also "take hold of . . . eternal life" (1 Timothy 6:12, NIV)—we grab it, setting our hope not on fleeting things, but on God, who gives eternal life and is himself hope.

Christ Provides Righteousness

GOD'S TRUTH

When we display our righteous deeds, they are nothing but filthy rags. *Isaiah 64:6*

I am overwhelmed with joy in the LORD my God! For he has dressed me with the clothing of salvation and draped me in a robe of righteousness. *Isaiah 61:10*

✿ If one of our young children came in from playing outside—covered from head to toe with mud—would we hand him a scrub brush and say, "Go to work on your clothes and clean off every last spot"? Of course not! We'd help clean him up and provide a fresh change of clothes. That's essentially what Jesus did for us by living a sinless life, dying on the cross to pay the price for our sin, and being raised from the dead. Because of what he did, every mom or child who trusts in Christ exchanges the rags of her sinfulness for Christ's righteousness!

God Can't Fail

GOD'S PROMISE

O Lord, our Lord, your majestic name fills the earth! Your glory is higher than the heavens. *Psalm 8:1*

He keeps every promise forever. *Psalm 146:6*

I will never fail you. I will never abandon you.
Hebrews 13:5

❀ While I rode in the car one day with five-year-old Chad, we talked about how strong God is. After discussing how God created all the animals, parted the waters of the Red Sea, and kept Daniel safe in the lions' den, I said, "There's nothing that God can't do." "Oh, yes there is," Chad piped up from the backseat. "God can't fail!" He got me on that one. God will never break his word or forsake us. No matter what kind of disappointment any of us has had or will ever experience, God will never fail us.

Gentle Words Are Effective

GOD'S WISDOM

A gentle answer deflects anger, but harsh words make tempers flare. *Proverbs 15:1*

Kind words are like honey—sweet to the soul and healthy for the body. *Proverbs 16:24*

Let everything you say be good and helpful, so that your words will be an encouragement to those who hear them.
Ephesians 4:29

❀ While in my thirties, I was hospitalized for a severe allergic reaction. I shared a hospital room with an elderly woman. I'll never forget the effect that the medical professionals' words had on the woman, confused though she was. Gentle and soft words, even when spoken firmly and directly, evoked a lot more cooperation from the woman than harsh, unpleasant ones. That principle holds true in dealing with our children, too. Words and tones that are considerate and compassionate will reap better results than words that are rough and strident.

Instruments for Good

GOD'S CHALLENGE

Do not let any part of your body become an instrument of evil to serve sin. Instead, give yourselves completely to God, for you were dead, but now you have new life. So use your whole body as an instrument to do what is right for the glory of God. *Romans 6:13*

❀ Scattered throughout my home are a piano, violin, trumpet, French horn, oboe, accordion, and several guitars. Each of these instruments is capable of producing beautiful music—or dreadful sounds, depending on how the instrument is played. The Bible tells us that our bodies are instruments too. They can be instruments of righteousness or instruments of evil. When we offer ourselves to God, he helps us use our bodies for his good purposes.

PRAYER

Father, I offer my body to you because I want to honor you. Thank you that you can use me for your glory! Amen.

Spending Time with Christ

GOD'S TRUTH

[Jesus said,] "There is only one thing worth being concerned about. Mary has discovered it, and it will not be taken away from her." *Luke 10:42*

The one thing I ask of the LORD—the thing I seek most—is to live in the house of the LORD all the days of my life, delighting in the LORD's perfections and meditating in his Temple. *Psalm 27:4*

❁ Mary from Bethany is seen three times in the Gospels, and in each scene she's sitting at the feet of Jesus. On one occasion she sits and listens to his Word (Luke 10:39). On another she falls at his feet and pours out her heart about the death of her brother, Lazarus (John 11:32). The third time she anoints Jesus' feet with expensive perfume (John 12:3). When we spend time in personal devotion to Christ, our acts of service—like Mary's—will flow out of grateful hearts.

Depend on God

GOD'S GUIDANCE
God is our refuge and strength, always ready to help in times of trouble. *Psalm 46:1*

You have been deceived by your own pride because you live in a rock fortress and make your home high in the mountains. "Who can ever reach us way up here?" you ask boastfully. *Obadiah 1:3*

❀ The Edomites—a nation of people neighboring ancient Israel—thought their mountain home was invincible, but it wasn't. The prophet Obadiah predicted their eventual judgment. It's easy for moms to make the same mistake by looking to power, wealth, or family heritage for our strength. But that's not where it's located. Our strength is found in God, and I'm thankful that he doesn't tire of my requests for his help.

PRAYER
Strong Father, thank you for always being ready to help us in times of trouble. We need your strength for the many challenges of motherhood. Amen.

Hands Can Bless

GOD'S ENCOURAGEMENT

Then [Jesus] took the children in his arms and placed his hands on their heads and blessed them. *Mark 10:16*

Jesus placed his hands on the man's eyes again, and his eyes were opened. His sight was completely restored, and he could see everything clearly. *Mark 8:25*

❀ When Jesus lived on earth, he used his hands to bless children, touch and heal the eyes of a blind man, and break loaves of bread for the hungry. A mother's hands can communicate blessing when they cuddle a baby or wipe away a toddler's tears. As the years pass, those same hands clap at ball games or recitals, prepare pizza for a birthday party, or fold in prayer as she pours out to God her concerns for a child's choices. Our hands can contribute to the growth of God's Kingdom in the lives of our families!

God Is Patient

GOD'S ASSURANCE

Has the Lord rejected me forever? Will he never again be kind to me? Is his unfailing love gone forever? Have his promises permanently failed? Has God forgotten to be gracious? Has he slammed the door on his compassion?

Psalm 77:7-9

✿ It's reassuring to me that these questions were asked by one of the psalmists. When I go through times of deep anguish, I sometimes wonder the same things. The verses of Psalm 77 move from crying, to pleading, to questioning, to despairing, to remembering. When the psalmist chooses to remember God's character and deeds, his perspective changes to worship! What a great pattern for moms. When we remember God's character and deeds, we come to the conclusion that God is always in control. Sometimes it takes a while to land on that assurance, but God is patient with us.

Jesus Deals with Us Gently

God's Comfort

Look at my servant, whom I strengthen. He is my chosen one, who pleases me. I have put my Spirit upon him. He will bring justice to the nations. . . . He will not crush the weakest reed or put out a flickering candle. *Isaiah 42:1, 3*

Have you ever felt so hurt by an unkind word that you could have burst into tears? Or have you felt so guilty about something you'd thought, said, or done that you found it hard to imagine that God could still love you? If so, then these images from Isaiah are for you! If you feel like a flickering candle, God will not come along and snuff you out. He will fan you into flame. If you feel like a broken reed, he won't tromp over you. He will pick you up and straighten you out. I'm thankful that Jesus deals gently with our fragile hearts.

God's Spirit Counsels Us

I will ask the Father, and he will give you another Counselor to be with you forever—the Spirit of truth. . . . The Counselor, the Holy Spirit, whom the Father will send in my name, will teach you all things and will remind you of everything I have said to you. *John 14:16-17, 26, NIV*

❀ Have you ever wished that you had your own personal counselor on call 24/7? If you have placed your faith in Christ, you do. As one of the three members of the Godhead, the Holy Spirit has the role of connecting believers with God. As we spend time in God's Word, the Holy Spirit comes alongside us to plant truth in our minds, convince us of God's will, and point out where we are straying from it. The Holy Spirit knows us, loves us, encourages us, is patient with us, and prays for us. What an awesome gift!

Victory in Christ

GOD'S HOPE

For you are my hiding place; you protect me from trouble.
You surround me with songs of victory. *Psalm 32:7*

For every child of God defeats this evil world, and we
achieve this victory through our faith. *1 John 5:4*

❁ Are you feeling overwhelmed with a particular challenge
today? Maybe it's finances . . . or your health . . . or your
troubled marriage . . . or your feelings of despair. Whatever
problem you may be facing, it's encouraging to learn that
the word *victory* shows up often in the Bible. Victory usually
includes an achievement or a triumph. It also involves the
crushing, squashing, or trampling of evil things. For believers, victory for any challenge we are dealing with comes
through faith in Christ.

PRAYER

Father, thank you that because of Christ, we have hope for victory! Amen.

October 11

Obedience Is Better Than a Compliment

God's Promise

As he was speaking, a woman in the crowd called out, "God bless your mother—the womb from which you came, and the breasts that nursed you!" Jesus replied, "But even more blessed are all who hear the word of God and put it into practice." *Luke 11:27-28*

When the woman in this story pronounced a blessing on Mary, she was also complimenting Jesus. But by Jesus' response we get the impression that he desires obedience more than compliments. Throughout God's Word we are taught that obedience comes after hearing. God has revealed his truth to us, and he asks us to respond to it positively and actively. Isn't that exactly what we desire from our children? Jesus used the word *blessed* in his response to the woman, meaning *happy.* When we hear God's Word and obey, that's true happiness.

Call Attention to Our Creator

GOD'S CHALLENGE

O LORD, our Lord, your majestic name fills the earth! Your glory is higher than the heavens. *Psalm 8:1*

Let every created thing give praise to the LORD, for he issued his command, and they came into being. *Psalm 148:5*

❀ I sometimes wonder how God feels when we go to the zoo and see all the animals he has created but forget to acknowledge him. I wonder how he feels when we walk outside late at night to observe the heavens, admiring the beauty of the moon and stars, but forget to praise him for designing and sustaining such beauty and glory. The next time we're admiring some of God's creation with our children, let's call attention to the Creator and give honor to him!

PRAYER

Father, may we be quick to praise you for your handiwork as we encounter it each day. Amen.

Giving God
Our Wholehearted Obedience

GOD'S TRUTH

King Rehoboam firmly established himself in Jerusalem and continued to rule. He was forty-one years old when he became king, and he reigned seventeen years in Jerusalem. . . . But he was an evil king, for he did not seek the LORD with all his heart. *2 Chronicles 12:13-14*

❀ While reading this morning in 2 Chronicles 12, I reflected on Rehoboam—a son of Solomon who became King of Judah. Although Rehoboam accomplished some good things, I felt sad when I read that "he abandoned the Law of the LORD, and all Israel followed him" (v.1). A whole nation may not be watching and following me, but my children are. That motivates me to obey God whole-heartedly.

PRAYER

Father, please give me the strength to obey you with my whole heart. I want to be a good example to my children. Amen.

Depend on God

GOD'S GUIDANCE

"Don't worry about this Philistine," David told Saul. "I'll go fight him!" "Don't be ridiculous!" Saul replied. "There's no way you can fight this Philistine and possibly win! You're only a boy, and he's been a man of war since his youth."

1 Samuel 17:32-33

❀ My sons loved the Old Testament story of David and Goliath. Humanly speaking, the battle plan didn't make any sense. Goliath was huge and should have won the fight easily, but in God's plan young David felled the giant with a single stone from his slingshot. We live in a highly competitive society that rewards the biggest and best. May we not be tricked into thinking that being strong and proud is good, and being weak and humble is bad. God's Word reminds us that dependence on God brings great success.

Trained for Battle

GOD'S ENCOURAGEMENT

He trains my hands for battle; he strengthens my arm to draw a bronze bow. You have given me your shield of victory. Your right hand supports me; your help has made me great. You have made a wide path for my feet to keep them from slipping. *Psalm 18:34-36*

❀ Moms of teenagers understand the phrase "trained for battle"! Although I enjoyed my sons' teenage years immensely, there were days when I felt that I was entering a battle zone. Even when we and our children follow Christ, we'll experience challenges and conflicts related to attitudes, modesty, friends, responsibility, and more. God never promised us that life would be easy, but he does promise to give us strength to face our challenges. He has also given us his Word to prepare us, fortify us, and uphold us. We don't need to do battle alone.

Praying with Groans

GOD'S ASSURANCE

The Holy Spirit helps us in our weakness. For example, we don't know what God wants us to pray for. But the Holy Spirit prays for us with groanings that cannot be expressed in words. And the Father who knows all hearts knows what the Spirit is saying. *Romans 8:26-27*

✾ Have you ever wanted to pray about a distressing or confusing matter, but you just didn't have the words? The Bible tells us that God's Spirit groans with us, sharing the burdens of our weakness and suffering. But he doesn't stop at groaning—he also prays for us! When I encounter situations that I cannot analyze or pray about intelligently, I plead for God's help, but I also rest in the assurance that the Holy Spirit is interceding for me.

PRAYER

Father, thank you that even when we can't find the words, your Spirit is gracious to pray for us. Amen.

Mercy, Not Sacrifices

GOD'S DIRECTION

I want you to show love, not offer sacrifices. I want you to know me more than I want burnt offerings. *Hosea 6:6*

"I want you to show mercy, not offer sacrifices." For I have come to call not those who think they are righteous, but those who know they are sinners. *Matthew 9:13*

❀ Sometimes it's easier for me to make a meal for someone I have little contact with than it is to show love to a family member who has hurt me. Sometimes it's easier for me to look at others and think how selfish they are than it is to look inside my heart and see my own bitterness. According to the verses above, God does not congratulate us for our righteousness and ask for our sacrifices. He wants us to admit that we're sinners, and he wants us to be willing to show his mercy to others.

God Intends It for Good

GOD'S DIRECTION

You intended to harm me, but God intended it all for good.
He brought me to this position so I could save the lives of
many people. *Genesis 50:20*

For I know the plans I have for you. . . . They are plans for
good and not for disaster. *Jeremiah 29:11*

❀ Sometimes our hardships are so big—or so persistent—
that we wonder, *Where is God's goodness in all of this?* Perhaps
the Old Testament character Joseph wondered the same thing
when he was sold into slavery by his brothers. But God's
goodness *was* there. God used Joseph's brothers' betrayal as
part of his plan to preserve the Israelites during a famine and
eventually lead them into the Promised Land. God works—
often behind the scenes—to bring good things out of difficult
situations. We can trust him to do that for *us!*

Peace of Mind and Heart

GOD'S PROMISE
A heart at peace gives life to the body, but envy rots the bones. *Proverbs 14:30, NIV*

Let the peace that comes from Christ rule in your hearts.
Colossians 3:15

[God's] peace will guard your hearts and minds as you live in Christ Jesus. *Philippians 4:7*

❀ Some recent scientific studies suggest that religious faith benefits health. The studies demonstrate to the world the truth of what the believer already knows: Our personal faith in God helps us grow in peace. The further we progress in our faith, the more settled we become. This isn't to say that we don't ever become sick, encounter serious problems in our families, or have anxious thoughts, but we have an anchor for our souls. Do things in your life feel out of control? Run to God. Run to his Word. To be in relationship with him is to experience peace.

Choosing Purity

GOD'S CHALLENGE

Don't let anyone think less of you because you are young.
Be an example to all believers in what you say, in the way
you live, in your love, your faith, and your purity.

1 Timothy 4:12

✿ "How can a young person stay pure?" Psalm 119:9 asks.
"By obeying your word" and following its rules. Purity also
comes to our hearts through cleansing. We come to God
asking him to create in us a new and clean heart. His promise in 1 John 1:9 assures us that he will: "But if we confess
our sins to him, he is faithful and just to forgive us our sins
and to cleanse us from all wickedness." Our responsibility is
to get rid of things that cause us to sin. God can use a willing and pure heart.

The Bible Transforms
Our Language

GOD'S TRUTH
All the nations of the world are but a drop in the bucket.
Isaiah 40:15

For the word of God is alive and powerful. It is sharper than the sharpest two-edged sword, cutting between soul and spirit, between joint and marrow. *Hebrews 4:12*

❀ Many clichés in our language had their beginning in the Bible. For example: Am I my brother's keeper? (Genesis 4:9); apple of my eye (Psalm 17:8); land of milk and honey (Exodus 3:8); casting pearls before swine (Matthew 7:6); as you sow, so shall you reap (Galatians 6:7); and don't let the left hand know what the right hand is doing (Matthew 6:3). So many people have been influenced by the Bible that its words have become part of our everyday idioms. God's Word is incredibly powerful. Not only does it direct us in our lives, but it has also transformed our language!

God Desires Our Attention

GOD'S GUIDANCE

And [the Israelites] said to Moses, "You speak to us, and we will listen. But don't let God speak directly to us, or we will die!" "Don't be afraid," Moses answered them, "for God has come in this way to test you, and so that your fear of him will keep you from sinning!" *Exodus 20:19-20*

✿ Sometimes we gain our children's attention simply by raising our eyebrows or clearing our throats. Other times, we need extra bells and whistles to do the job. God also uses various ways to get people's attention. Sometimes he speaks quietly; sometimes he displays amazing power. Whatever means he uses to get our attention, he wants us to see him for who he is and respond with reverent and affectionate obedience.

PRAYER

God, we're amazed at your awesome power. Help us to respond with reverence. In Jesus' name, amen.

God Is Our Protector

GOD'S ENCOURAGEMENT

Like an eagle that rouses her chicks and hovers over her young, so he spread his wings to take them up and carried them safely on his pinions. *Deuteronomy 32:11*

May the LORD, the God of Israel, under whose wings you have come to take refuge, reward you fully for what you have done. *Ruth 2:12*

Guard me as you would guard your own eyes. Hide me in the shadow of your wings. *Psalm 17:8*

❀ The "shadow of your wings" is a delightful picture that symbolizes God's great protection. Just as a mother bird guards her young by covering them with her wings, God *protects* us. Just as a mother eagle sometimes carries her eaglets on her wings, God *carries* us. His protection doesn't always remove us from difficult circumstances, but he promises to stay with us and guide us—even when things get tough.

Truth Brings Freedom

GOD'S ASSURANCE

To the Jews who had believed him, Jesus said, "If you hold
to my teaching, you are really my disciples. Then you will
know the truth, and the truth will set you free."

John 8:31-32, NIV

When the Spirit of truth comes, he will guide you into all
truth. *John 16:13*

❀ Who are Jesus' disciples? Who are people of the truth?
They are the people who obey God—the people who hold
to his teaching. Knowing the truth means accepting it,
obeying it, and regarding it above all earthly opinion.
Doing so offers true spiritual freedom from sin and death.
I'm thankful that discovering God's truth, obeying it, and
honoring it are not things we are asked to do on our own.
As believers, we have the Holy Spirit living within us to
guide us into all truth. As we obey the truth, we experience
freedom!

God Is Our Faithful Shepherd

GOD'S HOPE

I am the good shepherd. The good shepherd sacrifices his life for the sheep. *John 10:11*

My dear children, I am writing this to you so that you will not sin. But if anyone does sin, we have an advocate who pleads our case before the Father. He is Jesus Christ, the one who is truly righteous. He himself is the sacrifice that atones for our sins—and not only our sins but the sins of all the world. *1 John 2:1-2*

✤ Human beings can be a lot like sheep (moms and kids included). Because we sometimes wander off and get into trouble, we need a shepherd to follow. We need someone who cares for us and wants to show us—or graciously lead us back to—the right path. That's why God sent Jesus—to die for us, to forgive us, and to lead us.

God Is Worthy of Our Trust

GOD'S TRUTH

Can you direct the movements of the stars—binding the cluster of the Pleiades or loosening the cords of Orion? Can you direct the sequence of the seasons or guide the Bear with her cubs across the heavens? *Job 38:31-32*

❀ As moms, we do some tasks seasonally: We help our children prepare for school in the fall. We go Christmas shopping in the winter. We pick tulips in the spring and put away winter clothes. We sign our kids up for swimming lessons in the summer. Moms are capable of doing many things, but which of us could ever change the colors of the leaves, cause snow to fall on a quiet winter's night, prompt daffodils to spring up in March, or bring the cicadas around every seventeen years? God, who can order the seasons of the world without fail, is worthy of our trust!

Let Love Be Sincere

GOD'S GUIDANCE

We will speak the truth in love. *Ephesians 4:15*

Hate evil and love what is good. *Amos 5:15*

Don't just pretend to love others. Really love them. Hate what is wrong. Hold tightly to what is good. *Romans 12:9*

❀ Tucked away in Romans 12:9 is a marvelous little lesson about how to love people sincerely—even in difficult situations. The last two phrases outline it for us: "Hate what is wrong. Hold tightly to what is good." The guideline for loving a person who is involved in compromising behavior isn't to plaster a smile on our faces, ignore the problem, and feign love. Nor is it to blast away in a hateful way. Rather, it's to be lovingly straightforward. When we look to Christ, he helps us love sincerely because he is full of truth and grace!

PRAYER

Father, only you can help us find the right balance of truth and grace. Amen.

A Grateful Heart Spreads Cheer

God's Encouragement

Save us, O Lord our God! Gather us back from among the nations, so we can thank your holy name and rejoice and praise you. *Psalm 106:47*

Give thanks to the Lord, for he is good! His faithful love endures forever. *Psalm 107:1*

❁ Have you ever noticed that a grateful mom is not usually a miserable mom? I'm not suggesting that a grateful mom never gets sick, never gets angry at her kids, or never encounters challenges in relationships. But a grateful mom has an attractive manner that influences her family. Never underestimate the impact that your grateful heart will have on those around you!

Prayer

Father, we are grateful for your patience with us and the mercy you give. May we look for things to thank you for each day, rehearsing the blessings you have given us. Amen.

God Establishes Our Work

GOD'S ASSURANCE
Pay careful attention to your own work. *Galatians 6:4*

May the favor of the Lord our God rest upon us; establish the work of our hands for us—yes, establish the work of our hands. *Psalm 90:17,* NIV

✼ Moms invest hours of work in their children's lives—nursing, feeding, holding, singing, dressing, reading, doing puzzles, going to church, driving, hosting friends, cooking, praying, listening, talking, doing laundry, and providing music lessons. What a joy for moms to see their children growing, maturing, and accomplishing things on their own. It's especially meaningful to think that our work isn't aimed only at our children's life spans. When we are in relationship with the eternal God, our work is aimed toward eternity. That helps us understand what it means to see the work of our hands *established,* as Psalm 90:17 states.

PRAYER
Father, thank you for giving our work eternal impact. Amen.

Lies Destroy

GOD'S GUIDANCE

A deceitful tongue crushes the spirit. *Proverbs 15:4*

The LORD detests lying lips, but he delights in those who tell the truth *Proverbs 12:22*

Stop telling lies. Let us tell our neighbors the truth, for we are all parts of the same body. *Ephesians 4:25*

✿ "A little white lie never hurt anybody, right?" Actually, a lie does more than hurt—the Bible tells us that it "crushes the spirit." In addition to producing conflict and undermining relationships, lies can demolish friendships and marriages that have taken months or years to build. Several years ago, a house behind ours was knocked down. The original home, which had stood for about thirty years, took only two hours to raze once the demolition crew began. Sadly, lies and deceit can do the same to relationships. Next time you see a demolition site, remember that lies destroy—but the Bible promises that truth will set us free.

God Gives Good Gifts

GOD'S ENCOURAGEMENT

You fathers—if your children ask for a fish, do you give them a snake instead? Or if they ask for an egg, do you give them a scorpion? Of course not! So if you sinful people know how to give good gifts to your children, how much more will your heavenly Father give the Holy Spirit to those who ask him. *Luke 11:11-13*

❀ Immediately before surgery for a broken leg, our ten-year-old son looked up at my husband and me and asked us to buy him an electric guitar. You know the old saying, "Timing is everything"? We bought the electric guitar before Jordan even came home from the hospital! If we parents want to please our children and give them good gifts, how much more does God want to give his Spirit to those who ask?

PRAYER

Father, thank you for the gift of your Spirit, which gives us new life. Amen.

Elevated by Righteousness

GOD'S PROMISE

When calamity comes, the wicked are brought down, but even in death the righteous have a refuge. . . . Righteousness exalts a nation, but sin is a disgrace to any people.

Proverbs 14:32, 34, NIV

The LORD is the source of all my righteousness and strength.

Isaiah 45:24

❁ As we trust in Christ, he shares his righteousness with us. Our character becomes more like his, and our status is elevated—we become children of God. That's how righteousness *exalts* people. Christ's righteousness also *protects* us. Parents and children who choose to share the righteousness of Christ find refuge in him. He is a source of protection, shelter, help, relief, and comfort in times of trouble or hardship.

PRAYER

Father, thank you for sharing your righteousness with us. Amen.

What Is Heaven Like?

GOD'S HOPE

There is more than enough room in my Father's home. If this were not so, would I have told you that I am going to prepare a place for you? *John 14:2*

He will wipe every tear from their eyes, and there will be no more death or sorrow or crying or pain. All these things are gone forever. *Revelation 21:4*

✾ After my grandma died, my sister explained to three-year-old Brent that Great Grandma was in heaven with God and that she was very happy there. A few days later, after leaving Great Grandma's memorial service at a local funeral home, young Brent remarked, "I didn't think heaven would look like *that!*"

What is heaven like? Scripture tells us that heaven is where God is (Matthew 6:9), that Jesus has gone there ahead of us to prepare a place for us (John 14:2), and that it will be a safe and happy place (Revelation 21:3-4).

Consider the Outcome

GOD'S WISDOM

A prudent person foresees danger and takes precautions.
The simpleton goes blindly on and suffers the consequences.

Proverbs 22:3

You said, "I will reign forever as queen of the world!" You
did not reflect on your actions or think about their consequences. *Isaiah 47:7*

❀ *If I choose to do this, what might happen? If I pursue that
path, will there be any fallout?* One of my friends encouraged
her preschoolers to think this way when she told them stories
of children who tried "dancing" in the bathtub and ended up
knocking out a tooth, or a little girl who tried to cut her own
hair and ended up getting a short pixie cut. Whether we have
tots or teens, it's wise to teach them to anticipate the outcome
of their choices. It's a good idea for moms, too.

The Right Path

GOD'S CHALLENGE

I am the LORD your God, who teaches you what is good for you and leads you along the paths you should follow.

Isaiah 48:17

People with integrity walk safely, but those who follow crooked paths will slip and fall. *Proverbs 10:9*

❀ Several years ago, my husband and I and our three sons vacationed at a friend's cabin on Mount Princeton in Colorado. As we set out on a half-day hike to a peaceful mountain lake surrounded by fields of beautiful wildflowers, we were pumped! Somewhere along the way, though, we lost the path, wandered around on slippery slopes, encountered a thunderstorm, and came back wet and grumpy. We never even *saw* the lake or the beautiful flowers. The Bible warns us about experiences like that in our lives. Staying on the *right* path brings us peace and joy that we don't want to miss!

Tell of God's Provision

GOD'S TRUTH

Our children will also serve him. Future generations will hear about the wonders of the Lord. His righteous acts will be told to those not yet born. They will hear about everything he has done. *Psalm 22:30-31*

Let each generation tell its children of your mighty acts; let them proclaim your power. *Psalm 145:4*

❀ When my children were in the preschool and early elementary years, one of my favorite things to do was to read to them. Although we learned from many kinds of books, God's Word enriched us more than any other. Together we witnessed God's wonders and provisions in other people's lives—one of the many benefits of reading God's Word. We were encouraged to believe he would provide for us, too. Sometime this week, tell your child about a time in your life when God provided for *you*.

The Most Important Thing

GOD'S GUIDANCE

But how can they call on him to save them unless they believe in him? And how can they believe in him if they have never heard about him? And how can they hear about him unless someone tells them? *Romans 10:14*

Knowing God results in every other kind of understanding.
Proverbs 9:10, TLB

❀ It's important for moms to *protect* our children. It's important for moms to *teach* our children. It's important for moms to *love* our children. But the most important thing we can do for our children is to help them know God. Only by knowing God can our children understand themselves and the world around them. How do they get to know God? A great place to start is reading through one of the Gospels (Matthew, Mark, Luke, or John) or a Bible story-book about Jesus' life. Jesus teaches us that life in God's Kingdom is available through him!

God Is Our Ultimate Security

GOD'S ENCOURAGEMENT

Even if my father and mother abandon me, the LORD will hold me close. *Psalm 27:10*

Fear of the LORD leads to life, bringing security and protection from harm. *Proverbs 19:23*

But what joy for all who take refuge in [God]! *Psalm 2:12*

❁ How would you illustrate the word *security?* I might describe a little boy jumping into his father's arms, knowing that his dad would catch him—or I might envision a mother holding her sleeping baby snugly against her chest. Security is freedom from risk, danger, anxiety, or fear, and we mothers work at providing it for our children. Sadly, not all children grow up with this sense of security. No matter what kind of disappointment or rejection any of us has experienced, we know that if we come to God, he will *never* forsake us. Run into God's arms—he's *always* there!

Nothing Separates Us from God's Love

GOD'S ASSURANCE

I am convinced that nothing can ever separate us from God's love. . . . No power in the sky above or in the earth below—indeed, nothing in all creation will ever be able to separate us from the love of God that is revealed in Christ Jesus our Lord. *Romans 8:38-39*

❀ One of the small luxuries in my life is brewing a pot of coffee once or twice a day. I drop a few tablespoons of coffee grounds into a filter and let the grounds soak in boiling water until the coffee drips into the serving carafe, ready for me to drink. The filter separates the coffee grounds from the hot water so I don't end up with grounds in my cup. Separation is important when it comes to coffee grounds. When it comes to God's love, though, I'm thankful that nothing—*nothing*—can ever separate me from God's love!

God's Peace Is Available under All Circumstances

GOD'S COMFORT

I have told you all this so that you may have peace in me. Here on earth you will have many trials and sorrows. But take heart, because I have overcome the world. *John 16:33*

I am leaving you with a gift—peace of mind and heart. And the peace I give is a gift the world cannot give. *John 14:27*

✿ Many people think of peace as the absence of conflict, but Jesus taught a different kind of peace. He never claimed that we would experience only times of quiet. In fact, our enemy, the devil, seeks to destroy us and undermine our faith, and as long as we are alive, we are in a battle. The peace that Jesus brings is a combination of hope, trust, and quiet in our minds and souls. We can experience it no matter what our circumstances are.

Rejoice When the Truth Wins Out

GOD'S DIRECTION

[Love] rejoices whenever the truth wins out.

1 Corinthians 13:6

Everything I [wisdom] say is right, for I speak the truth and detest every kind of deception. *Proverbs 8:6-7*

Truthful words stand the test of time, but lies are soon exposed. *Proverbs 12:19*

❀ My cousin Al's wife, Lori, recently discovered—at the age of fifty-nine—that she had been adopted when she was seven months old. "I grew up thinking I was Italian," Lori shared, "but now I've learned that I'm really Czechoslovakian." In Lori's case, withholding information redefined her whole life. But now that she has met seven siblings she never knew she had, Lori is thankful that the secret has been uncovered. As my mom used to say to me, "Honesty is the best policy."

God Gives Power, Stability, and Vitality

GOD'S ENCOURAGEMENT

I love you, LORD; you are my strength. The LORD is my rock, my fortress, and my savior . . . in whom I find protection. He is my shield, the power that saves me, and my place of safety. I called on the LORD, who is worthy of praise, and he saved me from my enemies. *Psalm 18:1-3*

❀ It's encouraging that the psalmist found God to be his rock in the midst of adversaries, rebels, and traitors. After all, moms need the same thing. We need God to be our power, stability, and vitality in the face of the neighborhood bully, a rebellious teenager, or a husband who has strayed from God's truth. I'm reassured to know that God heard the psalmist and helped him. When we call on him, he will provide strength for us, too.

Good News

GOD'S HOPE

The Spirit of the LORD is upon me, for he has anointed me to bring Good News to the poor. He has sent me to proclaim that captives will be released, that the blind will see, that the oppressed will be set free, and that the time of the LORD's favor has come. *Luke 4:18-19*

❀ This passage demonstrates salvation's balance between grace and truth. The truth is that we're all poor, but the grace is that God has given us *his* riches. On our own we're all prisoners to sin, but Christ brings freedom. The truth is that, left to ourselves, we are spiritually blind, but the grace is that God can give us sight. We are oppressed, but by faith in Jesus' death for us, we can be released and protected. God's gracious salvation makes us rich!

Look to God for Protection

GOD'S PROMISE

The LORD is my light and my salvation—so why should I be afraid? The LORD is my fortress, protecting me from danger, so why should I tremble? *Psalm 27:1*

God's way is perfect. All the LORD's promises prove true. He is a shield for all who look to him for protection.
Psalm 18:30

❀ David, the author of Psalm 27, faced many harrowing experiences. Chased by jealous King Saul, David spent some of his early years as a leader running from one rocky mountain to the next, trying to stay one step ahead of his challenges. Motherhood can sometimes feel like that! But David reminds us that the Lord is our light and our salvation—so why should we fear? We, too, can claim God's promises that he will take care of us.

PRAYER

Lord, thank you for being our Protector. In Jesus' name, amen.

Encourage Someone Today

GOD'S CHALLENGE

But encourage one another daily, as long as it is called Today, so that none of you may be hardened by sin's deceitfulness. *Hebrews 3:13,* NIV

Strengthen those who have tired hands, and encourage those who have weak knees. *Isaiah 35:3*

❀ Encouragement—how do we do it? To begin with, we come alongside others with listening, understanding, and help. When we're concerned, we can pray that we'll have an appropriate balance of truth and grace. Sharing God's Word is another way to inspire one another to possess hope and courage. When my children are going through difficulties, I sometimes jot down for them specific Bible verses I am praying regarding their circumstances. This can also be helpful for husbands, for friends, and for ourselves. How can we encourage someone today?

PRAYER

Father, thanks for the encouragement we have received from fellow believers in times of personal disappointment. Amen.

What's Most Important?

GOD'S TRUTH

You are careful to tithe even the tiniest income from your herb gardens, but you ignore the more important aspects of the law—justice, mercy, and faith. You should tithe, yes, but do not neglect the more important things. . . . You strain your water so you won't accidentally swallow a gnat, but you swallow a camel! *Matthew 23:23-24*

❀ Sometimes we pour liquids (like tea) or mixtures (like gravy) through a sieve or strainer to remove larger particles. In the Gospel of Matthew, Jesus used hyperbole—or exaggeration—when he contrasted the pictures of straining out a gnat and swallowing a camel. He wanted the scrupulous Pharisees to see that in focusing on details, they were missing the main points—justice, mercy, and faith. As we look to God for his perspective on our lives, we'll be able to focus on what's most important to him!

God Grants Wisdom

GOD'S GUIDANCE

Guide my steps by your word, so I will not be overcome by evil. *Psalm 119:133*

For the LORD grants wisdom! From his mouth come knowledge and understanding. *Proverbs 2:6*

I will guide you along the best pathway for your life.
Psalm 32:8

❀ A young man who hoped to be chosen as a steamboat pilot on the Mississippi River was nearing the end of his job interview. The interviewer, wondering if the young man was aware of the dangers of the river, asked if he knew where all the rocks were. The young man wisely responded, "No, sir, but I know where they *aren't.*" As moms, we need help navigating the river of motherhood. Help is available in the form of God's words, which show us the safe paths. His words are something we need to hear every day of motherhood—even after our kids have left home!

Don't Give Up! Look to Jesus

GOD'S ENCOURAGEMENT

As pressure and stress bear down on me, I find joy in your commands. *Psalm 119:143*

If you fail under pressure, your strength is too small.
Proverbs 24:10

Think of all the hostility [Jesus] endured from sinful people; then you won't become weary and give up. *Hebrews 12:3*

❀ Pressure. Stress. Difficulty. None of us like it, but all moms face it. The writer of Hebrews gave us wise and help-ful words for such times. He didn't say, "Focus on yourself." He didn't suggest, "Concentrate on your circumstances." He said that if we want to deal effectively with tension in our lives, we must keep our eyes on Jesus—the One who initiates and perfects our faith (see Hebrews 12:2). If we keep our eyes on him, we won't lose sight of the big picture. Besides that, he promises us his presence and his help!

The Supreme Counselor

GOD'S ASSURANCE

You guide me with your counsel, leading me to a glorious destiny. Whom have I in heaven but you? I desire you more than anything on earth. My health may fail, and my spirit may grow weak, but God remains the strength of my heart; he is mine forever. *Psalm 73:24-26*

❀ Where we look for guidance says a lot about our character. Some people turn to the local bar or a palm reader, but we're wise to turn to a mature person who loves God and his Word. Although human counselors are helpful, Jesus is the foremost counselor in the world. He knows us, loves us, is patient with us, and encourages us. And—like any good counselor—he doesn't protect us from problems, but he equips us to face them with honesty and courage. When you need direction, grab on to Jesus' hand and ask *him* to help you.

Pitch a Tent!

GOD'S HOPE

For we know that when this earthly tent we live in is taken down (that is, when we die and leave this earthly body), we will have a house in heaven, an eternal body made for us by God himself and not by human hands. *2 Corinthians 5:1*

✿ A tent is designed to be put up for a short period of time and quickly dismantled. In comparison to the homes we live in, a tent is a temporary, flimsy structure. The Bible likens our bodies on earth to tents but our bodies in heaven to houses. With all their problems and limitations, our earthly bodies are temporary. I'm grateful that our heavenly bodies—perfect, glorious, and without limitations—will last forever!

PRAYER

Father, when life seems hard, help me to remember what is temporary and what is eternal. Amen.

You Are Valuable

GOD'S ENCOURAGEMENT

What is the price of five sparrows—two copper coins? Yet God does not forget a single one of them. And the very hairs on your head are all numbered. So don't be afraid; you are more valuable to God than a whole flock of sparrows.

Luke 12:6-7

✾ Jesus taught that God cares about each sparrow, and that each of us is worth much more than a sparrow to him. Too many times we judge our worth by what we believe others think of us—depending on how we look or how well we perform. When we look to God for our worth, though, we receive from him a deep sense of belonging. Moms need that! It gives us great comfort to know that if God cares for even the most common of birds, he most certainly cares for us.

A Day of Rest

GOD'S TRUTH

There is a special rest still waiting for the people of God. For all who have entered into God's rest have rested from their labors, just as God did after creating the world. So let us do our best to enter that rest. But if we disobey God, as the people of Israel did, we will fall. *Hebrews 4:9-11*

✿ Why rest one day each week? Our bodies need a break from the routine of work. Our souls need strength—so we worship with other believers and spend time in fellowship. Our emotions need refreshment—so we focus on different things than we do the rest of the week. Beyond this, God has commanded us to rest, and when we obey his commands, we demonstrate submission to his authority. Resting becomes a step of faith as we trust God to help us accomplish in six days what might otherwise take seven days each week.

PRAYER

Father, thank you for knowing our needs and providing a day of rest. Amen.

Pray Anytime and Anywhere!

GOD'S GUIDANCE

We keep on praying for you, asking our God to enable you to live a life worthy of his call. May he give you the power to accomplish all the good things your faith prompts you to do. *2 Thessalonians 1:11*

We always thank God for all of you and pray for you constantly. *1 Thessalonians 1:2*

❀ Mark Twain once said, "I don't know of a single foreign product that enters this country untaxed except the answer to prayer." Whether our children are in our house, down the street, or around the world, we can communicate with God on their behalf, having confidence that God sees their bodies, minds, and hearts. Prayer, unlike long-distance phone calls, does not cost money. We don't have to shop around for the best rates. We can talk to God anytime!

PRAYER

Father, thank you for always hearing us. Amen.

God Renews Us

GOD'S ENCOURAGEMENT
He renews my strength. He guides me along right paths,
bringing honor to his name. *Psalm 23:3*

I long to obey your commandments! Renew my life with
your goodness. *Psalm 119:40*

That is why we never give up. Though our bodies are dying,
our spirits are being renewed every day. *2 Corinthians 4:16*

❀ My brother and his wife recently purchased a condominium in Hallandale, Florida. Before they could move in,
though, it needed major renewal. The walls had termite
damage, the bathrooms and kitchen needed to be over-
hauled, and the whole place needed new paint. They hired
a contractor to remodel the unit, and now it sparkles! Our
hearts sometimes need renewal too. They need to be refur-
bished, restored, and transformed. I'm grateful that God is
willing to renew us through *his* goodness.

Examples of Comfort

GOD'S ASSURANCE

All praise to God, the Father of our Lord Jesus Christ. God is our merciful Father and the source of all comfort. He comforts us in all our troubles so that we can comfort others. . . . We are confident that as you share in our sufferings, you will also share in the comfort God gives us.

2 Corinthians 1:3-4, 7

❀ A month before my friend Marty died of cancer, she gave me a copy of the book *A Shepherd Looks at Psalm 23.* The author's wife had been sick with cancer for two years before she died, and he wrote, not as one untouched by difficulty, but rather as one who had walked through pain and loss himself. Do we want the valleys? No! But when we experience God's faithfulness and comfort even in the valleys, we can be living examples to others.

Hope for Our Challenges

GOD'S HOPE

Your eternal word, O LORD, stands firm in heaven. . . . I will never forget your commandments, for by them you give me life. . . . You are my refuge and my shield; your word is my source of hope. *Psalm 119:89, 93, 114*

❀ My high school son's girlfriend had just broken up with him. When I walked upstairs to check on him, the first thing I noticed was his red eyes. The second thing I noticed was his open Bible. When I asked him what he was reading, he said, "Hebrews 13:5, where God promises that he will never leave us or forsake us." Then it was my turn to get misty eyes. I was reminded of why it's important to saturate our children's lives with reverent knowledge of God's Word. Then, when they need hope and encouragement, they'll know exactly where to go.

The Best Advice

GOD'S TRUTH

Who is able to advise the Spirit of the LORD? Who knows enough to give him advice or teach him? Has the LORD ever needed anyone's advice? Does he need instruction about what is good? Did someone teach him what is right or show him the path of justice? *Isaiah 40:13-14*

❀ Where do you go when you need advice? It probably depends on what kind of advice you're looking for. If your drain is clogged, you call a plumber. If your car needs to be repaired, you call the auto technician. If you're ill, you call a physician. Isaiah 40:13-14 helps us to see that God is the *only* One in the universe who doesn't need someone to offer him a recommendation or give him a tip. Because he is all-knowing, totally powerful, and completely just, we are wise to run to him whenever we need advice.

Keep on Praying!

GOD'S GUIDANCE
Never stop praying. *1 Thessalonians 5:17*

So we keep on praying for you, asking our God to enable you to live a life worthy of his call. May he give you the power to accomplish all the good things your faith prompts you to do. *2 Thessalonians 1:11*

Be patient in trouble, and keep on praying. *Romans 12:12*

❁ Did you ever play Ding-Dong Ditch when you were a kid? In this prankish game, a child rings a doorbell and promptly runs out of sight before the homeowner can get to the door. I wonder if we're sometimes like that child when it comes to our prayers. We pray, but then we promptly move on to other things. What might happen if we "stayed on the doorstep" or prayed with perseverance? Today, think of one specific concern for your child that you're going to *keep* praying about, no matter what!

God Delights in You

GOD'S ENCOURAGEMENT
He will take great delight in you. *Zephaniah 3:17, NIV*

The LORD your God will delight in you if you obey his voice and keep the commands and decrees written in this Book of Instruction, and if you turn to the LORD your God with all your heart and soul. *Deuteronomy 30:10*

❀ While my baby nursed for as long as a feeding took (some seemed to take forever), I delighted in him. I enjoyed studying my little one's face and experiencing eyeball-to-eyeball contact—especially when he smiled. What a picture of contentment! What does it mean for God to delight in us? It means that he takes pleasure in us. He appreciates us, cherishes us, and enjoys us. Not only is that how a nursing mother feels toward her baby, but—according to this verse—it's how God feels toward us!

Find Strength, Courage, and Wisdom in Christ

GOD'S ASSURANCE

For God in all his fullness was pleased to live in Christ.

Colossians 1:19

For in Christ lives all the fullness of God in a human body. So you also are complete through your union with Christ, who is the head over every ruler and authority.

Colossians 2:9-10

Have you ever gone to the refrigerator and reached for milk, only to discover that the bottle is empty? We'd much rather find a bottle of milk that's *full.* We long for fullness in our souls, too, and God's Word assures us that satisfaction is found in Christ. The next time your soul feels empty of strength, wisdom, or courage, run to Christ. Because he *is* the fullness of God, when we draw on Christ, we are filled with the fullness of God!

Long-Distance Vision

GOD'S HOPE

My eyes are straining to see your promises come true.
Psalm 119:82

My eyes strain to see your rescue, to see the truth of your promise fulfilled. *Psalm 119:123*

The Scriptures give us hope and encouragement as we wait patiently for God's promises to be fulfilled. *Romans 15:4*

❀ The first clue that one of our children needs to visit the eye doctor often comes from a teacher who reports, "Your child seems to be straining her eyes to see the blackboard." Her long-distance vision might need to be corrected. Sometimes our hearts strain to see God's promises come true, and long-distance vision adjustments are helpful then. When I look into Scripture and see what God has done in the past, I gain encouragement and hope for the present and the future. Just as God's promises proved true for Abraham, Joshua, and Ruth, they will prove true for me.

Whom Do You Reflect?

GOD'S PROMISE

But we all, with unveiled face, beholding as in a mirror the glory of the Lord, are being transformed into the same image from glory to glory, just as from the Lord, the Spirit.

2 Corinthians 3:18, NASB

❀ A reflector is a surface that bounces light back. Almost every object reflects some light, although a dark surface reflects hardly any. But a shiny surface like a mirror reflects almost all the light that shines on it. Christian moms have the privilege of reflecting (reproducing or copying) God's glory to our families as we gaze on the Lord and live in his light. The more of God's nature we come to know and experience, the more we will reflect him to our children.

PRAYER

Father, thank you that we can reflect your glory. Amen.

Constructive Consequences

GOD'S CHALLENGE

Discipline your children while there is hope. Otherwise you will ruin their lives. *Proverbs 19:18*

Don't fail to discipline your children. *Proverbs 23:13*

Joyful are those you discipline, LORD, those you teach with your instructions. *Psalm 94:12*

❀ It's good for moms to be empathetic to the pain and feelings of our kids. When children are experiencing the natural consequences of their destructive behavior, though, it's not healthy for us to step in and protect them. If we do, we're basically encouraging more of the same behavior in the future. Part of our role as mothers is to help our children see that their behavior, good or bad, has consequences. And it's much better for them to learn that in the small things now than to experience great difficulties with higher authorities down the road.

PRAYER

Lord, please give me wisdom as I discipline my children. Amen.

Protect Your Heart

GOD'S CHALLENGE

Guard your heart above all else, for it determines the course of your life. *Proverbs 4:23*

Love the LORD your God with all your heart, all your soul, and all your strength. *Deuteronomy 6:5*

Store my commands in your heart. *Proverbs 3:1*

❀ We make sure that our drinking water is clean and sanitized. But over the course of our lives, how protective are we about the purity of our hearts—and our children's hearts? Proverbs 4:23 cautions us to guard our hearts above everything else. To keep our hearts pure, we need to ask God for his help, be accountable to others, avoid tempting situations, and spend time in God's Word.

Pure drinking water is good, but pure hearts are more important. "Put everything into the care of your heart," wrote Dallas Willard, "for it determines what your life amounts to."

PRAYER

Father, thank you for caring so much about our hearts. Amen.

Faith Fortifies Us

GOD'S TRUTH

The local residents tried to discourage and frighten the people of Judah to keep them from their work. They bribed agents to work against them and to frustrate their plans. This went on during the entire reign of King Cyrus of Persia and lasted until King Darius of Persia took the throne.

Ezra 4:4-5

❀ How often do you feel frustrated in your role as a mom? Maybe it's only once in a while—but on a particularly challenging day with toddlers, it could be twice an hour! It's helpful for us to identify these potentially paralyzing feelings, name them, and run to God, his Word, and his people for fortification and encouragement. Through time spent with God and time spent with other believers in Christ, our souls are nourished so that we can keep doing the good work God has placed before us.

Wise Moms Listen

GOD'S GUIDANCE
Wise people treasure knowledge, but the babbling of a fool invites disaster. *Proverbs 10:14*

My child, listen and be wise: Keep your heart on the right course. *Proverbs 23:19*

Listen as Wisdom calls out! Hear as understanding raises her voice! *Proverbs 8:1*

❀ I used to think that if I wasn't talking, I was listening. But I'm learning that listening is making an *effort* to hear something, and paying close attention in the process. Listening is a gift we moms can give to our children. Although it doesn't cost money, it does cost time. If our children don't receive focused attention from us, the message they receive is that everything else is more important than they are. But when we put other things aside and listen to our children, they feel valued and important. We can practice that skill today!

PRAYER
Father, help us to become active, empathetic listeners. Amen.

Aim toward Christ

GOD'S ENCOURAGEMENT

Whenever I pray, I make my requests for all of you with joy. . . . And I am certain that God, who began the good work within you, will continue his work until it is finally finished on the day when Christ Jesus returns.

Philippians 1:4, 6

❁ As a child, Colin Smith spent hours playing with his battery-operated toy boat. Lying prostrate at the edge of a pond in Edinburgh, Scotland, he would aim the boat in the "perfect" direction, and let it go. "The funny thing," he said, "was that it never ended up going exactly where I aimed it." Other forces were at work—the wind above the water and the weeds beneath the water. Raising children is a lot like that. But if we aim our children toward Christ and trust them to his care, he will do a much better job of getting them through the wind and the weeds than we ever could.

Greater Is He That Is in You

GOD'S ASSURANCE

He has rescued us from the kingdom of darkness and transferred us into the Kingdom of his dear Son, who purchased our freedom and forgave our sins. *Colossians 1:13-14*

You have already won a victory . . . , because the Spirit who lives in you is greater than the spirit who lives in the world.
1 John 4:4

❀ "Greater is he that is in you, than he that is in the world." Sometimes I sing this phrase during times of fear and doubt. Part of a little chorus I learned as a child, these words bring hope to my heart. Why? Because God's victory over Satan's deathly power was accomplished through Jesus' death and resurrection. And the same victory over fear and doubt is accomplished in our hearts *as we trust in Christ!*

God Cares for Me Like a Shepherd

GOD'S COMFORT
I myself will tend my sheep. *Ezekiel 34:15*

I am the good shepherd. *John 10:14*

He will feed his flock like a shepherd. He will carry the
lambs in his arms, holding them close to his heart. He will
gently lead the mother sheep with their young. *Isaiah 40:11*

❀ The words from Isaiah 40:11 have been set to gorgeous
music by George Frideric Handel in *Messiah*. The first time
I heard the piece sung by alto and soprano soloists, I was
moved to tears—partly, I think, because of the nurturing
instinct God has placed inside me. To this day, I am awed
to think that the overwhelming desire I had as a young
mom to carry, hold, and protect my defenseless babies is
like God's desire to carry, hold, and protect me.

Our Shepherd Cares for Us

GOD'S DIRECTION

The LORD is my shepherd; I shall not want. He makes me to lie down in green pastures; He leads me beside the still waters. He restores my soul; He leads me in the paths of righteousness for His name's sake. *Psalm 23:1-3, NKJV*

❀ A little boy was once heard misquoting this verse. He said, "The Lord is my shepherd—what more shall I want?" He had the right idea. Sheep are the most frequently mentioned animals in the Bible, and we humans sometimes have a lot in common with them! We are stubborn, we tend to follow the crowd, we are fearful, and we sometimes get into things that we shouldn't. Like sheep, we need someone to follow. At times when we feel confused and uncertain, we can thank God that he is our Shepherd who knows us and provides for us.

Hope through the Gospel

GOD'S HOPE

With this news, strengthen those who have tired hands, and encourage those who have weak knees. Say to those with fearful hearts, "Be strong, and do not fear, for your God is coming to destroy your enemies. He is coming to save you."

Isaiah 35:3-4

✽ *Are you tired?* Be strengthened. *Are you weak?* Be encouraged. *Are you fearful?* Be assured. The words of hope that Isaiah spoke seven hundred years before Christ continue to give us hope today. There *is* a place where no more sorrow or mourning will exist. There *is* a place where everything will be joy and gladness. There *is* a place where disabilities will disappear. How do we get there? The Bible's answer to all who would follow God on this Highway of Holiness (see Isaiah 35:8) is *through faith in Christ*. Be encouraged as you follow him.

Jesus Is Patient with Our Doubts

GOD'S PROMISE

[Jesus] said to Thomas, "Put your finger here, and look at my hands. Put your hand into the wound in my side. Don't be faithless any longer. Believe! . . . You believe because you have seen me. Blessed are those who believe without seeing me." *John 20:27-29*

❀ Although Thomas was one of Jesus' disciples, he struggled to believe that Jesus had really risen from the dead. Sometimes moms have doubts too. *Will God really take care of my child? Will he really help me?* Thomas's struggle for faith offers us hope. If Jesus showed patience to Thomas and a willingness to help him believe, he will do the same for us. And in John 20:29, Jesus offers "extra credit" to the person who believes *without* seeing. God's Word—and the witness of people like Thomas—inspires us to believe.

God's Creative Pleasure

GOD'S TRUTH
The birds nest beside the streams and sing among the branches of the trees. . . . There the birds make their nests, and the storks make their homes in the cypresses. . . . May the glory of the LORD continue forever! The LORD takes pleasure in all he has made! *Psalm 104:12, 17, 31*

❀ I can't imagine what it's like for God to know and enjoy *everything* he created. Take white storks, for example. They live mostly in Eastern Europe and Western Asia, and they winter in Africa. Although they look striking in flight, they're not physically suited for a long journey over the open sea. Consequently, they travel to Africa by way of Gibraltar or Istanbul. I'm thankful that we'll have all eternity to praise God for the many wonders of his creation—a few of which we're privileged to know and see now!

Jesus Is Our Pattern

GOD'S GUIDANCE

Don't be selfish; don't try to impress others. Be humble, thinking of others as better than yourselves. . . . You must have the same attitude that Christ Jesus had. Though he was God, he did not think of equality with God as something to cling to. *Philippians 2:3, 5-6*

✻ I've yet to run across a book titled *Humility 101* in my local bookstore. It's just not a popular subject in the self-help section. So where do we go if we want to learn how to be humble? In Philippians 2, we discover that humility begins with Jesus. Instead of demanding service, Jesus served. Instead of clinging to his rights, he thought about others. Moms have opportunities to make these choices hourly! If we choose the attitude of humility that Jesus had, the actions of humility will likely follow.

PRAYER

Jesus, I want to follow your perfect example of humility. Amen.

Bless Your Children

GOD'S ENCOURAGEMENT

May the LORD bless you and protect you. May the LORD smile on you and be gracious to you. May the LORD show you his favor and give you his peace. *Numbers 6:24-26*

May the LORD richly bless both you and your children.
Psalm 115:14

❀ The words we speak to our children hold tremendous influence on their future. Here are a few ways to encourage your children to look for God's blessings: (1) when a child has had a bad day at school, pray together that God will bring some special blessing or encouragement to that child's life—and thank him together when he does; (2) as a son or daughter displays characteristics that will be admirable in marriage or parenthood someday, affirm them; (3) pray the verses above for your child at bedtime or when he or she is leaving on a trip.

PRAYER

Lord, help me to speak wise, affirming words to my children. Amen.

Remember God's Faithfulness

GOD'S HOPE

Why am I discouraged? Why is my heart so sad? I will put my hope in God! I will praise him again—my Savior and my God! Now I am deeply discouraged, but I will remember you—even from distant Mount Hermon, the source of the Jordan, from the land of Mount Mizar. *Psalm 42:5-6*

❀ When the author of Psalm 42 felt discouraged, he first asked two "why?" questions. After his questions, he made some good choices. One was to remember God. I recall a time in my life when I was deeply discouraged and struggling for hope. I decided to take a walk to town and back (one hour, round trip) and rehearse some of God's provisions to me. By the time I returned home, I had a more hopeful perspective. Remembering God's faithfulness in the past gives us a hopeful boost for the present.

Advantages of Fearing God

GOD'S PROMISE

Praise the LORD! How joyful are those who fear the LORD and delight in obeying his commands. Their children will be successful everywhere; an entire generation of godly people will be blessed. They themselves will be wealthy, and their good deeds will last forever. *Psalm 112:1-3*

❀ I recently purchased a box of Frosted Mini-Wheats cereal that advertised, "Take the Kellogg's 2-week Fiber Challenge. Try it & see if you feel a difference." I tried it, and although I don't feel much different, I do like the cereal! The promises contained in Psalm 112 hold much more hope for me than those on the cereal box. Psalm 112 states an impressive list of advantages for those who fear God and delight in his commands: joy, children's successes, blessings to an entire generation, wealth, light, no need to fear bad news, confidence, influence, and honor. Fearing God does make a difference!

Ambassadors of Christ

GOD'S TRUTH

We are Christ's ambassadors; God is making his appeal through us. We speak for Christ when we plead, "Come back to God!" For God made Christ, who never sinned, to be the offering for our sin, so that we could be made right with God through Christ. *2 Corinthians 5:20-21*

✿ Moms can be ambassadors of the Good News—first to our children, and then to others we meet. Our daily briefing on God's plan for the world comes through the time we spend in his Word. The message we have been given is that through Christ we can have a relationship with God. Because of that relationship, God's Spirit lives in us and helps us to represent God effectively and tactfully. We are messengers of peace. What a privileged position we hold!

Crave Spiritual Milk

GOD'S GUIDANCE

Like newborn babies, you must crave pure spiritual milk so that you will grow into a full experience of salvation. Cry out for this nourishment, now that you have had a taste of the Lord's kindness. *1 Peter 2:2-3*

Is anyone thirsty? Come and drink—even if you have no money! Come, take your choice of wine or milk—it's all free! *Isaiah 55:1*

❀ When my sons were newborns, it seemed like they were always hungry! Hunger was an instinct they were born with, and their cries communicated the feeling quite effectively. They *craved* milk. It wasn't unusual for them to nurse from both breasts, take a brief nap, and then wake up wanting to nurse again. Craving isn't just for babies, though. To grow spiritually, we need to crave God's Word. It feeds and nourishes us—both young believers and mature believers—and it's free for the taking.

Witnesses to Faith

GOD'S ENCOURAGEMENT

Therefore, since we are surrounded by such a huge crowd of witnesses to the life of faith, let us strip off every weight that slows us down, especially the sin that so easily trips us up. And let us run with endurance the race God has set before us. *Hebrews 12:1*

Although the Bible assures me that I am "surrounded by such a huge crowd of witnesses to the life of faith," I know that the enemy wants me to feel lonely and discouraged. Sometimes I do. As I near the end of writing this book, I have about ten devotionals to go. But yesterday, I felt dry and inadequate for the task. My sister Barb called, and when I shared my downheartedness with her, she listened, encouraged me with Psalm 77, and prayed for me over the phone. God can encourage us with the love of even *one* witness to the life of faith!

What to Expect

GOD'S HOPE

For they keep talking about the wonderful welcome you gave us and how you turned away from idols to serve the living and true God. And they speak of how you are looking forward to the coming of God's Son from heaven—Jesus, whom God raised from the dead. He is the one who has rescued us from the terrors of the coming judgment.

1 Thessalonians 1:9-10

❀ Several years ago, I came across a book in Barnes & Noble's family section titled *What to Expect When You're Expecting. What a great title,* I thought. *Where was that book when I was pregnant?* First Thessalonians 1:9-10 seems to be a "what to expect" guide for the believer in Christ. If we've placed our faith in Christ's death and resurrection and accepted God's forgiveness, we can expect to see some distinguishing characteristics: turning away from God-substitutes, serving God, and waiting for Christ's return. There's a lot to look forward to!

God Transforms

GOD'S ASSURANCE

The angel replied, ". . . The baby to be born will be holy, and he will be called the Son of God. . . . For nothing is impossible with God." *Luke 1:35, 37*

[Jesus] replied, "What is impossible for people is possible with God." *Luke 18:27*

❁ The angel's announcement of the virgin birth had the word *impossible* written all over it. Mary was young and unmarried, and she hadn't experienced sexual relations. But Mary's response to the angel was incredible. She didn't say, "This is impossible!" She said, "How will this be?" In response, the angel announced that the Holy Spirit would overshadow her, and she would experience the transforming power of God's presence.

Are you facing an impossible situation? Do circumstances seem insurmountable? Be encouraged! As believers, we too have the presence of God's Spirit, who specializes in transforming our hearts—even in difficult situations.

Humility Focuses on Christ

GOD'S TRUTH

Mary responded [to Elizabeth], "Oh, how my soul praises the Lord. How my spirit rejoices in God my Savior! For he took notice of his lowly servant girl, and from now on all generations will call me blessed. For the Mighty One is holy, and he has done great things for me." *Luke 1:46-49*

❀ Humility jumps from the page as we read about Mary reflecting on God's promise to make her the mother of the Messiah. What are some characteristics of a humble heart?

1. Humility moves the focus off ourselves. Mary didn't praise herself—she praised God.
2. Humility doesn't mean insecurity. Mary felt God's power and love for her.
3. Humility looks at the big picture. Mary understood that she was part of a much bigger plan than just her days on earth.

PRAYER

Father, help me to focus on you and follow Mary's example of humility. Amen.

God Has Purposes for Our Inconvenience

All returned to their own ancestral towns to register for this census. And because Joseph was a descendant of King David, he had to go to Bethlehem in Judea, David's ancient home. He traveled there from the village of Nazareth in Galilee. He took with him Mary, his fiancée, who was now obviously pregnant. *Luke 2:3-5*

❀ Imagine being pregnant and traveling eighty miles on a donkey—to pay taxes! This inconvenient trip was a small part of God's divine plan for the ages. Although Joseph and Mary traveled to Bethlehem because of the Roman Empire's law, God was really in control. Are you experiencing some inconvenience or tragedy in your family that doesn't make sense to you? Be encouraged that God often takes difficult things that don't make sense to us and weaves them into purposes we don't yet see.

God's Good Plan Sometimes Includes Reversals

GOD'S DIRECTION

"Joseph, son of David," the angel said, "do not be afraid to take Mary as your wife. For the child within her was conceived by the Holy Spirit. And she will have a son, and you are to name him Jesus, for he will save his people from their sins." *Matthew 1:20-21*

❀ To think that the Creator of the universe was about to be born of a peasant virgin on cold stable ground is astonishing. Jesus' entrance into our human existence was one of the greatest reversals of all time. Perhaps you have experienced difficult turnarounds that don't seem to make sense to you. God sometimes uses reversals in our lives as part of his plan to accomplish great things and deliver good news to all people.

PRAYER

Father, thank you for not shunning the reversal of dying for our sins. Amen.

Dignity in Humility

GOD'S ENCOURAGEMENT

After seeing him, the shepherds told everyone what had happened and what the angel had said to them about this child. . . . The shepherds went back to their flocks, glorifying and praising God for all they had heard and seen. It was just as the angel had told them. *Luke 2:17, 20*

Whom did God choose to tell first about his son's birth? Shepherds! An angel of the Lord appeared to humble shepherds who were tending their sheep underneath the night sky. How encouraging! God doesn't seek people with extraordinary qualifications. He seeks people who are quietly doing their jobs, and uses those people for his purposes. That brings a lot of dignity to our roles as moms, doesn't it? We can serve God right where we are.

PRAYER

Father, like the humble shepherds, we want to worship and serve you too. Amen.

Jesus Brings Light

GOD'S PROMISE

[The Lord] has raised up a horn of salvation for us . . . to give to His people the knowledge of salvation by the forgiveness of their sins, because of the tender mercy of our God, with which the Sunrise from on high will visit us, to shine upon those who sit in darkness and the shadow of death. *Luke 1:69, 77-79, NASB*

❀ "The Sunrise from on high" is one image used to describe Jesus' birth. In a tender moment, Simeon took the child in his arms and said that he was ready to die, now that God's promise to him had been fulfilled and he had seen Jesus, *the Light.* Like Simeon, we can place our faith in Jesus. And when we experience his sunrise in our souls, we'll want to point our children to Christ too.

Divine Purposes

GOD'S GUIDANCE

At that time there was a man in Jerusalem named Simeon.
He was righteous and devout and was eagerly waiting for
the Messiah to come and rescue Israel. The Holy Spirit was
upon him and had revealed to him that he would not die
until he had seen the Lord's Messiah. *Luke 2:25-26*

❀ Simeon was eager for Jesus to bring light to all people,
and as a result of his righteous and devout life, he was ready
to be used at just the right time for God's divine purposes.
How encouraging! As moms, we have opportunities every
day to bring God's light to our children through his Word
and through his love. Who knows what divine purposes he
is accomplishing in us and for us?

PRAYER

Father, please help us fulfill your purposes. In the name of
Jesus, amen.

Words That Strengthen

GOD'S WISDOM

The lips of the godly speak helpful words, but the mouth of the wicked speaks perverse words. *Proverbs 10:32*

Kind words are like honey—sweet to the soul and healthy for the body. *Proverbs 16:24*

A gossip goes around telling secrets, but those who are trustworthy can keep a confidence. *Proverbs 11:13*

❀ I remember one exciting Christmas as a child when one of my younger sisters received a Chatty Cathy doll. If we pulled the cord on the doll's back, she spoke preset sentences. What fun we had! In real life, of course, God has not programmed us with only a few phrases that we must repeat throughout our lives (although our kids might accuse us of repetition sometimes). He gave us the freedom of language, and we are privileged to choose words that will encourage and strengthen our children!

Perfect Praise? Only in Heaven

GOD'S TRUTH

Give thanks to the LORD, for he is good! His faithful love endures forever. Has the LORD redeemed you? Then speak out! Tell others he has redeemed you from your enemies. . . . Let them praise the LORD for his great love and for the wonderful things he has done for them.

Psalm 107:1-2, 8

❀ One of the more memorable word slips of our two-year-old son, Chad, was his version of a children's praise song. Instead of "Praise him, praise him, all ye little children," he sang, "Praise him, praise him, *naughty* little children." One of our friends remarked, "Well, he does have his theology straight." Only in heaven does God hear perfect praise. If we wait until we are "good enough" to offer something to God, praise will never happen. Isn't that exactly why we praise him? We praise God for providing forgiveness, healing, and hope for us all.

All Things Work for Good

GOD'S HOPE

And we know that God causes everything to work together for the good of those who love God and are called according to his purpose for them. *Romans 8:28*

Because we are united with Christ, we have received an inheritance from God, for he chose us in advance, and he makes everything work out according to his plan.

Ephesians 1:11

❁ Have you experienced a period in your life that included disappointment, loss, or pain? At the time, things probably didn't make sense to you, and your predominant thought might have been, *Surely nothing good can ever come out of this!* I'm thankful to have lived long enough to see God use painful circumstances to accomplish good things in my heart. When difficult situations challenge you, remember these verses and be encouraged to trust him more.

New Strength

GOD'S ENCOURAGEMENT

He gives power to the weak and strength to the powerless. Even youths will become weak and tired, and young men will fall in exhaustion. But those who trust in the LORD will find new strength. They will soar high on wings like eagles. They will run and not grow weary. They will walk and not faint. *Isaiah 40:29-31*

✿ Eagles are majestic birds, and the God who created them knows the address of every eagle alive. An eagle can soar for hours at a time while searching for prey. It rides wind currents, rarely moving its wings. God promises us that if we hope in him, he will provide some of that soaring time as well. Sometimes we soar, sometimes we run, sometimes we walk, and sometimes we stumble and fall. But the Lord offers us new strength as we hope in him.

Index

God's Guidance

God's Wisdom

Other One Year® Mini Devotionals

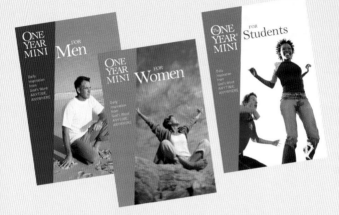

Through Scripture quotations and a related devotional thought, *The One Year Mini for Men* helps men connect with God anytime, anywhere between their regular devotion times. Hardcover ISBN-10: 1-4143-0618-0; ISBN-13: 978-1-4143-0618-6

The One Year Mini for Women helps women connect with God through several Scripture verses and a devotional thought. Perfect for use anytime, anywhere between regular devotion times. Hardcover ISBN-10: 1-4143-0617-2; ISBN-13: 978-1-4143-0617-9

The One Year Mini for Students offers high school and college students an anytime, anywhere connection with God, helping them stay grounded through the ups and downs of their busy lives. Hardcover ISBN-10: 1-4143-0619-9; ISBN-13: 978-1-4143-0619-3

You might also enjoy
these full-size
One Year® Devotionals

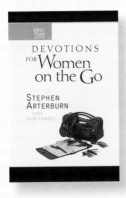

*The One Year® Book
of Devotions for Women,*
by Jill Briscoe

Softcover
ISBN-10: 0-8423-5233-3
ISBN-13: 978-0-8423-5233-8

*The One Year® Book
of Devotions for Women
on the Go,*
by Stephen Arterburn
and Pam Farrel.

Softcover
ISBN-10: 0-8423-5757-2
ISBN-13: 978-0-8423-5757-9